Knit One BEAD Too

Knit One BEAD Too

Essential Techniques
for Knitting with Beads

JUDITH DURANT

Storey Publishing

The mission of Storey Publishing is to serve our customers by
publishing practical information that encourages
personal independence in harmony with the environment.

Edited by Gwen Steege and Kathy Brock
Art direction and book design by Mary Winkelman Velgos
Text production by Jennifer Jepson Smith

Photography and illustration credits appear on page 158

Tech edited by Amy Polcyn
Indexed by Christine R. Lindemer, Boston Road Communications

Printed in China by SNP Leefung Printers Limited
10 9 8 7 6 5 4 3 2 1

Library of Congress Cataloging-in-Publication Data

Durant, Judith, 1955–
   Knit one, bead too / by Judith Durant.
        p. cm.
   Includes bibliographical references and index.
   ISBN 978-1-60342-149-2 (hardcover with concealed wire-o : alk. paper)
   1. Knitting. 2. Beadwork. I. Title.
TT825.D7695 2009
746.43'2—dc22
                                      2009007801

This book is dedicated to
knitters and beaders everywhere
who continue to innovate
and share ideas.

To present the techniques in this book, I've picked up
the threads of countless knitters and beaders, known and
unknown, past and present. The history of knitting is
somewhat vague: The oldest surviving fragments of knitted cotton are from Egypt and date to somewhere around
1000 AD.

The history of beads begins much earlier than that of
knitted fabric. The first known beads, made from animal
teeth and bones, were discovered in France, at an archaeo-
logical site called La Quina, and date to approximately
38,000 BC. Bead manufacture has come a long way over
the past 40,000 years, and today beads are made in every
conceivable shape and size and from materials ranging
from wood to glass to plastic to metal to clay.

I wish I could tell you who first had the brilliant idea
to knit with beads, but that history is a bit elusive. The
best theory seems to be that it developed from needlepoint, where one bead is incorporated into each stitch of
the work to "paint" a picture. One example dates to the
beginning of the nineteenth century, and there are many
examples of the technique used for gloves, bonnets, and
purses from 1850 onward.

— *Judith Durant*

Contents

(continued on page 9)

Contents *(continued)*

The Best of Both Worlds

If there's any such thing as "the best of both worlds," I'd have to say that this is it. Many of us who love to knit are also drawn to beads and beadwork, and now we can do beadwork on our knitting needles!

There are two distinct ways to incorporate beads into your knitting projects: You can add beads to a finished knitted piece as fringe, embroidery, or appliqué; or you can incorporate beads into the knitting as you go. This book will focus on the latter, and there are several techniques you can use. The first two techniques are traditional, dating back to at least the midnineteenth and early twentieth centuries respectively, and the last three are more recent developments. All but the last technique require that you pre-string beads onto your yarn.

Bead Knitting

Bead knitting (chapter 2) is the technique to use for pictorial designs. It was popular with Victorian-era knitters and was used in baby bonnets, gloves, socks, handbags, and other small items. While you may use the technique for one-color and random designs, for pictorial designs you'll have to pre-string the beads according to a chart. Bead knitting is done on a stockinette-stitch background, and each bead is knitted or purled into a stitch.

Beaded Knitting

With beaded knitting, (chapter 3) a bead (or beads) lies on the thread between two stitches. With this technique you can actually shape your knitted piece by adding more beads, and it is the method that was used in many 1920s beaded purses. The beads are usually all one color, so pre-stringing is a lot easier than for bead knitting with a chart. Beads lying between two knit stitches show on the back of the work; beads lying between two purl stitches show on the front of the work. Shaped pieces like the beaded purses are done in garter stitch, and beads are incorporated on both sides of the fabric.

Slipstitch Bead Knitting

Slipstitch bead knitting (chapter 4) leaves a bead floating on top of a slipped stitch, and you can use the technique to add a bead on top of a knitted or a purled stitch. Beads may be placed randomly or in a pattern, and because the bead lies on top of the fabric it will not affect your gauge. When you get to the place where you want a bead, you bring the yarn to the front, slide one bead up close to the needle, slip the stitch, and work the next stitch. You may place a bead on the front side when working either right- or wrong-side rows.

Carry-Along Bead Knitting

Another option is carry-along bead knitting (chapter 5). With this method, you string beads onto a separate thread that you carry along with your main yarn. This affords you the possibility of knitting with beads that are too small to thread onto your knitting yarn. You also can use large beads with this method. Because the beads are on a separate thread, they will not affect your gauge.

Hook Bead Knitting

Finally, with hook bead knitting (chapter 6) you can add beads to individual stitches with a crochet hook. With this method, no pre-stringing is necessary. When you get to the place where you want a bead, you place a bead on a small crochet hook, remove the stitch from the knitting needle, pull it through the bead, and then replace the stitch on the knitting needle. This can save wear and tear on delicate yarn.

In the chapters that follow, you'll find detailed instructions for these five techniques, along with projects that use each one. (Each project contains an alternate suggestion for beads and yarn.) I hope you will be inspired to incorporate beads into your own unique designs. Have fun knitting with beads!

① Tools and Techniques

If you're a knitter, you know how many different yarns are available, ranging in weight from super fine to super bulky, and in fibers from wool to cotton to silk to rayon to bamboo to soy to too many to name!

If you're a beader, you know the same holds true with beads. Beads range in size from miniscule seed beads to large pendants and are made from acrylic, crystal, glass, gemstones, metal, wood, and more. In fact, anything with a hole for stringing can be considered a bead.

Once you get started knitting with beads, it'll be difficult to see an end to your options. This chapter details some suggestions to get you started.

BEADS

A few important things to consider when selecting beads to knit with are weight, smoothness, and finish. There's no question that too many beads can make a garment uncomfortably heavy and also stretch the fabric. Beads that have sharp edges should be avoided because they can fray or cut your yarn. There are also beads out there that look terrific in their little vials, but they have finishes that can rub off over time and affect the appearance of your garment. Most of the beads used in this book are seed beads made from glass, as detailed in the choices that follow.

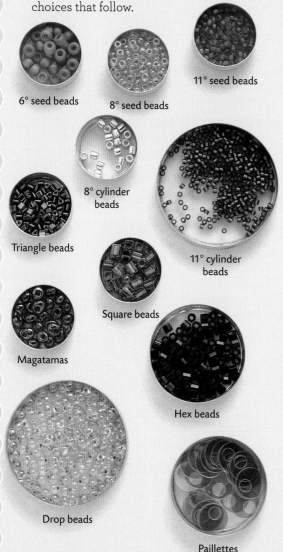

6° seed beads

8° seed beads

11° seed beads

8° cylinder beads

Triangle beads

11° cylinder beads

Square beads

Magatamas

Hex beads

Drop beads

Paillettes

Bead Shapes and Sizes

Japanese and Czech seed beads come in sizes ranging from 20° to 6°. The larger the number, the smaller the bead. The projects in this book use sizes 11°, 10°, 8°, and 6°.

Cylinder beads are tubular in shape and have a larger hole than regular seed beads, making them ideal for knitting. They are commonly available in sizes 11° and 8°, and size 10° has more recently come on the market.

Cut beads have one or more facets, which add to the shine. Beads with three sides are called **triangles,** and beads with six sides are called **hex. Square beads** are also available.

Drop beads look like seed beads with an off-center hole. Size 4mm drop beads are called **magatamas** and look like 6° seed beads with an off-center hole.

Paillettes look like large, plastic sequins with an off-center hole. You'll need the large-hole version for knitting, and they are generally available in 10mm and 20mm sizes.

Seed Bead Colors and Finishes

Seed beads are available in many colors and finishes. The color/finish choices shown here are those used for the projects in this book.

Transparent beads are made of colored glass that lets light shine through. Be aware that the color of your thread can change the color of your bead. This is not necessarily a bad thing. One of the Carpet Coasters (see page 32), for example, uses transparent topaz beads on red thread. The result is that the bead appears to be a shade of red when viewed straight on, but when viewed from an angle, the bead "turns" topaz.

Opaque beads are a solid color that doesn't let light through; therefore, the yarn color won't affect the bead's appearance. Opaque beads can be shiny or matte.

Iridescent beads seem to change color when viewed from different angles.

Lined beads shine from the inside out. They may be clear or colored, and the lining may be a dyed color, silver, or gold. I love these beads for knitting, but you should use them only on yarn that is thin enough to allow them to slide without being pushed. Pushing lined beads along the yarn can wear the lining right off.

Metal and metallic beads are very tempting to work with, but many of them have surfaces that will rub off or dull through contact with skin oils or dry-cleaning chemicals. Check with your bead shop or the manufacturer to find out what to expect in terms of durability.

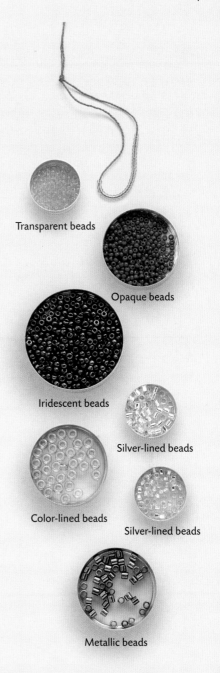

Transparent beads

Opaque beads

Iridescent beads

Silver-lined beads

Color-lined beads

Silver-lined beads

Metallic beads

YARN

Yarn used for knitting with beads needs to be strong and durable. Most importantly, it needs to be thin enough to accommodate your beads. Here's a rough idea of what will work.

·· **Size 8 perle cotton, size 20 crochet cotton, size E silk,** and **lace-weight yarn** all work well for bead knitting with 11° seed beads. Silk will last a lot longer but is also much more expensive.

·· **Size 5 perle cotton, size 10 crochet cotton, size FF silk,** and most **fingering yarns** are compatible with 8° seed beads.

·· **DK and sport-weight yarn** will accommodate 6° seed beads and many other novelty beads such as paillettes.

Note: These are guidelines only — all beads are not created equal. Unfortunately, one 8° seed bead may not have the same size hole as an 8° seed bead with a different finish or from a different manufacturer. If possible, check your yarn and beads for compatibility before making your purchases.

KNITTING NEEDLES AND HOOKS

There are no special needle requirements for knitting with beads — just use whatever you'd use without the beads. For bead knitting with small seed beads, choose steel needles, which come in sizes 00000 through 0, with 0 being the largest. Size 00 works well with size 10 crochet cotton and 8° seed beads, as in the Turquoise Mixed Bag (see page 36), and size 0000 is the choice for 11° seed beads and size 8 perle cotton, as in the Carpet Coasters (see page 32).

For hook bead knitting, choose steel crochet hooks for small seed beads. These hooks range in size from 00 to 14, with 14 being the smallest. Any size crochet hook that will fit through your bead and pick up a stitch will work.

BEADING SURFACES

You'll need a cloth surface to pour your beads onto, so they won't roll off the table while stringing. My favorite type is made with Vellux fabric, but you could also use a piece of terry cloth or felt. Once your beads are strung, you won't need the cloth as you knit the project, but if you're hooking, you should have your beads on a cloth and at-the-ready when you need them.

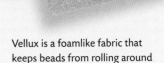

Vellux is a foamlike fabric that keeps beads from rolling around

WINDING YARN

It is very important to rewind your yarn before beginning to string beads. There is nothing more maddening than pushing the beads down the yarn only to find them stopped because there's a knot in the yarn.

If you're using a ball winder, loosely hold the yarn with your idle hand, letting it run through your fingers on its way to the winder. If you discover a knot, stop winding, cut the yarn at the knot, and begin a new ball. You'll have to estimate how many beads to string on your partial balls, but it's better than having to stop the knitting and transfer the beads from one ball to another. (Obviously, you should also cut out any knots from yarn you are rewinding by hand.)

If you run into a knot in the yarn when winding, cut it out and begin a new ball.

A finer yarn or thread is used as an intermediary loop when stringing beads into heavier-weight yarn.

PRE-STRINGING BEADS

For all of the techniques, except hook bead knitting, you'll need to pre-string the beads onto the yarn. I like to use big eye beading needles, which come in 2⅛" (5.5 cm) and 4½" (11.5 cm) lengths. The needle is split down the center, creating an eye that's almost as long as the needle and will accommodate any yarn.

When you're doing pictorial bead knitting, you'll have to string the beads in order according to a chart (see pages 26–29). To string large quantities of either same-color beads or random mixes, pour the beads out onto a beading surface (see Beading Surfaces, page 19) and pick them up from there, or pour them into a shallow bowl and scoop them up. Either way, pick up the beads with the needle; don't pick up a bead with your hand and place it on the needle because this method is tedious and takes a very long time.

If the bead hole is too small to slide over a big eye beading needle and doubled yarn, try using an intermediary loop of thread between the needle and the yarn. Thread a beading needle with a length of fine, strong thread. Tie the ends into a small knot, forming a loop. Thread the knitting yarn through the loop of thread. Now string beads onto the needle, slide them over the interme-diary thread, then onto the knitting yarn, as shown in the photo above.

You may find that you need a firmer grip on the needle than you can get with your bare hands to get the beads started onto the yarn. Simply grasp the needle with a pair of needle-nose pliers with one hand, and slide the beads onto the yarn with the other.

Determining How Many Beads to String

You'll want to estimate how many beads you'll need on each skein of yarn. The best way to do this is by swatching.

Once you've chosen your pattern and determined where you're going to place beads, string a few dozen beads and knit a 4" (10 cm) square swatch. If you're satisfied with the result, count the beads, undo the knitting, and measure the length of the yarn. Let's say you have 10 yards (9 meters) of yarn and you used 20 beads. That's two beads per yard, so if the ball of yarn is 160 yards (146 meters) long, you'll need to string 320 beads on each ball. Rather than counting the beads out, string a 4" (10 cm) length of

beads and count them. If you're using 8° seed beads, there should be about 44, or 11 beads per inch. Divide the total number of beads required by 11 to learn how many inches of beads to string. In the given example, you'd string about 29" (74 cm) of beads.

No matter what the math says, I usually don't string more than 6 or 7 yards (5.5 or 6.5 meters) of beads at a time, unless I'm using a strong yarn with beads that easily slide along it. That's because when you start knitting, you'll have to continually push the beads down the length of the yarn to pull up enough yarn to form stitches. This process can be tedious with too many beads, and all the extra pushing can take a toll on your yarn.

TAMING STRUNG BEADS

After the beads are strung, your knitting project once again becomes portable. However, if you just toss everything into your knitting bag, you could end up with a tangled mess. I use a separate project bag when knitting with beads, one that has nothing in it but my beaded yarn.

To keep the unknitted yarn from unwinding from the ball and becoming entangled with the strung beads, place the ball in a ziplock plastic bag and close the bag, leaving only a small opening for the yarn to come through. Toss the plastic bag in your knitting bag and let the strung beads pool around in the bottom of the bag. When you need to push the beads down the yarn, the beads will stay outside the plastic bag where they won't interfere with the yarn ball.

② Bead Knitting

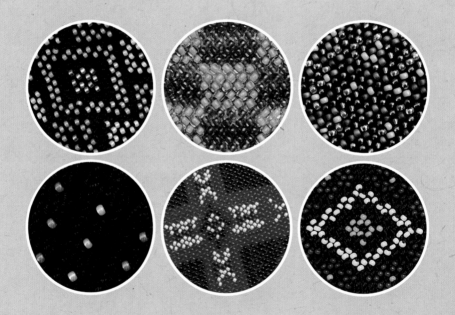

Traditional bead knitting, which dates back at least to the midnineteenth century, calls for a bead to be knitted into a stitch as it is worked. Beads may be worked into all of the stitches, as in the Carpet Coasters (see page 32), or into only some of the stitches, as in the Colorful Diamonds Gloves (see page 40).

Bead knitting is worked in stockinette stitch, and you can work circularly or flat, incorporating beads into both knit and purl stitches.

The work emulates needlepoint and often follows a pictorial chart in the same manner. However, unlike needlepoint, where you pick up and incorporate beads one at a time, with bead knitting, you pre-string the beads for the project before you begin to knit. If you're not following a chart, as in the Turquoise Mixed Bag (see page 36), simply string beads randomly. If you're knitting from a chart, you'll have to string the beads according to the chart. One bead should be about the same size as one knit stitch. Because it is difficult to keep edge beads in line, always include at least one or two nonbeaded edge stitches on each side of beaded motifs.

PREVENTING BIAS SKEW

▲ Because the beads sit at an angle on one-half of a stitch, knitting back and forth in the "normal" way will cause the finished fabric to skew on the bias.

▲ This bias occurs with both flat and circular bead knitting. This sample is knit in the round with plain, unbeaded stitches on the back.

▲ To prevent the fabric from biasing, you can twist the stitches in every other row of the work. When knitting back and forth,

you may simply work the knit rows through the back loop and work the purl rows as usual. This method may make the fabric lean slightly in the opposite direction.

▲ You also may work the knit rows in the Eastern method (so-called because it is the method used in Eastern Europe) and work the purl rows as usual. I think using this method produces the best results: The work does not lean one way or the other.

When knitting circularly, work every other row in one of these twisted methods and work alternate rows as usual.

Note how the flower motif changes appearance, depending on the knitting method used. When all rows are knit in the usual way, the beads are all tipped in the same direction and line up with each other like tiles. When a twisted method is used to compensate for bias, the beads in every other row tilt in the opposite direction, making beads in a vertical line zigzag somewhat, rather than run in a straight line.

KNITTING WITH A BEAD

▲ **To work a regular knit stitch,** ① insert the needle into the front of the stitch as usual, wrap the yarn around the needle, and slide a bead up against the needle. ② Push the bead through the stitch on the needle as you knit the new stitch.

▲ **To work a knit stitch through the back loop,** ① insert the needle into the back of the stitch, and wrap the yarn around the needle, sliding a bead up against the needle. ② Push the bead through the stitch on the needle as you knit the new stitch.

▲ **To work a knit stitch in the Eastern method,** ① insert the needle into the back of the stitch, and wrap the yarn around the needle from front to back, sliding a bead up against the needle. ② Push the bead through the stitch on the needle as you knit the new stitch.

PURLING WITH A BEAD

▲ **Insert the needle into the stitch** ① from back to front as usual, wrap the yarn around the needle, and slide a bead up against the needle. ② Push the bead through the stitch on the needle to the front of the work as you purl the new stitch.

READING CHARTS

There are many charted designs for stranded knitting, needlepoint, and other crafts that can be used for bead knitting. Whether you'll be knitting back and forth or in the round, the beads must be strung so the last bead you put on the yarn is the first bead you add to your knitting. Let's say you want to knit this flower (chart on facing page). The charted motif is 17 stitches wide by 16 rows tall.

Knitting Back and Forth

The knitting will begin at the lower right corner of the chart, and knit rows are worked from right to left, while purl rows are worked from left to right. Since the chart has an even number of rows, the last row worked will be a purl row. This means that the last bead knitted will be the bead in the upper right corner, so that's where the stringing begins.

For stringing, all even-numbered rows are read from right to left and odd-numbered rows are read from left to right. Working back and forth, string the beads in the following order:

- **ROW 16:** 17 white.
- **ROW 15:** 8 white, 3 red, 2 white, 2 red, 2 white.
- **ROW 14:** 2 white, 3 red, 1 white, 3 red, 8 white.
- **ROW 13:** 9 white, 2 red, 1 white, 3 red, 2 white.
- **ROW 12:** 4 white, 1 red, 1 white, 1 red, 1 white, 4 red, 5 white.
- **ROW 11:** 5 white, 5 red, 2 yellow, 2 white, 2 red, 1 white.
- **ROW 10:** 1 white, 4 red, 2 yellow, 2 white, 2 red, 6 white.
- **ROW 9:** 1 white, 1 green, 7 white, 1 red, 1 white, 1 red, 1 white, 3 red, 1 white.
- **ROW 8:** 4 white, 2 red, 1 white, 2 red, 1 white, 2 green, 3 white, 1 green, 1 white.

- ROW 7: 2 white, 3 green, 2 white, 3 red, 1 white, 3 red, 3 white.
- ROW 6: 3 white, 3 red, 1 white, 3 red, 1 white, 2 green, 4 white.
- ROW 5: 4 white, 3 green, 10 white.
- ROW 4: 10 white, 3 green, 4 white.
- ROW 3: 5 white, 2 green, 10 white.
- ROW 2: 10 white, 1 green, 6 white.
- ROW 1: 17 white.

The beads are now in the correct order for knitting, with the last bead strung being the first bead to go into the project. Now you may simply knit away, working a bead into every knit and every purl stitch.

For *stringing* beads for back-and-forth knitting

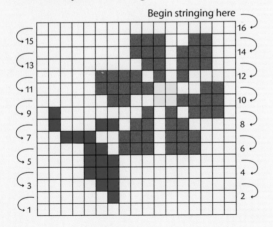

Begin stringing here

For *knitting* back and forth

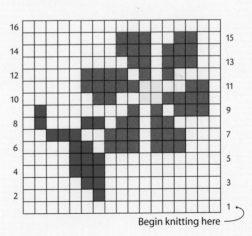

Begin knitting here

Knitting Circularly

The knitting will begin at the lower right corner of the chart, and all rows are followed from right to left. This means that the last bead knitted will be the bead in the upper left corner, so that's where the stringing begins. When stringing, read all chart rows from left to right. Working circularly, string the beads in the following order:

- **ROUND 16:** 17 white.
- **ROUND 15:** 8 white, 3 red, 2 white, 2 red, 2 white.
- **ROUND 14:** 8 white, 3 red, 1 white, 3 red, 2 white.
- **ROUND 13:** 9 white, 2 red, 1 white, 3 red, 2 white.
- **ROUND 12:** 5 white, 4 red, 1 white, 1 red, 1 white, 1 red, 4 white.
- **ROUND 11:** 5 white, 5 red, 2 yellow, 2 white, 2 red, 1 white.
- **ROUND 10:** 6 white, 2 red, 2 white, 2 yellow, 4 red, 1 white.
- **ROUND 9:** 1 white, 1 green, 7 white, 1 red, 1 white, 1 red, 1 white, 3 red, 1 white.
- **ROUND 8:** 1 white, 1 green, 3 white, 2 green, 1 white, 2 red, 1 white, 2 red, 4 white.
- **ROUND 7:** 2 white, 3 green, 2 white, 3 red, 1 white, 3 red, 3 white.
- **ROUND 6:** 4 white, 2 green, 1 white, 3 red, 1 white, 3 red, 3 white.
- **ROUND 5:** 4 white, 3 green, 10 white.
- **ROUND 4:** 4 white, 3 green, 10 white.
- **ROUND 3:** 5 white, 2 green, 10 white.
- **ROUND 2:** 6 white, 1 green, 10 white.
- **ROUND 1:** 17 white.

The beads are now in the correct order for knitting, with the last bead strung being the first bead to go into the project.

*For **stringing** beads for circular knitting*

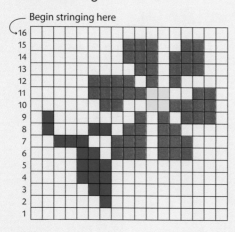

Begin stringing here

*For **knitting** circularly*

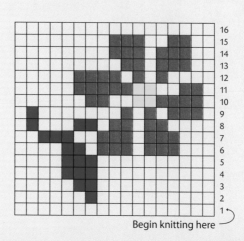

Begin knitting here

Knitting with a Plain Background

The white background can either be filled with white beads, or those stitches may be knit without beads. The same principles hold for stringing as for the examples just given: the last bead strung is the first bead to go into the project. When reading the chart, simply skip the white beads and string only the colored beads. To work the flower with a plain background back and forth, string beads in the following order:

- ROW 16: 0.
- ROW 15: 5 red.
- ROW 14: 6 red.
- ROW 13: 5 red.
- ROW 12: 6 red.
- ROW 11: 5 red, 2 yellow, 2 red.
- ROW 10: 4 red, 2 yellow, 2 red.
- ROW 9: 1 green, 5 red.
- ROW 8: 4 red, 3 green.
- ROW 7: 3 green, 6 red.
- ROW 6: 6 red, 2 green.

- ROW 5: 3 green.
- ROW 4: 3 green.
- ROW 3: 2 green.
- ROW 2: 1 green.
- ROW 1: 0.

Because the background stitches are not beaded, you'll have to read the chart while knitting to get the beads in the right place. For example, the first few rows are knit as follows:

- ROW 1: K17.
- ROW 2: P6, purl 1 with bead, P10.
- ROW 3: K10, knit 2 with beads, K5.
- ROW 4: P4, purl 3 with beads, P10.

*For **stringing** beads with plain background*

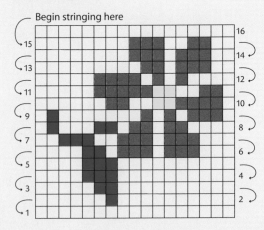

*For **knitting** back and forth (plain background)*

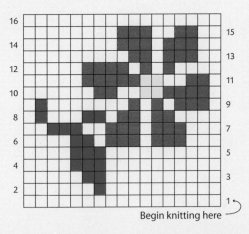

CORRECTING MISTAKES

No matter how hard you try to get it right, mistakes can happen in bead knitting. And as with most knitting mistakes, ripping back and re-knitting is the best cure. Depending on the type of mistake, though, there are a few other possibilities.

Stringing Errors

When following a chart, it is crucial that you string the beads in the correct order for knitting. Always do this work when you can concentrate, uninterrupted, for a period of time. If you have to stop before finishing, mark your chart so you know exactly what to do next. It's also not a bad idea to check each row when you've finished, just to be sure.

That said, mistakes in stringing do happen. If you're lucky enough to have simply strung one extra bead, you may carefully crush it with a pair of pliers to remove it and go on your merry way. If your pliers have serrated surfaces, wrap the ends in masking tape so you won't fray the yarn.

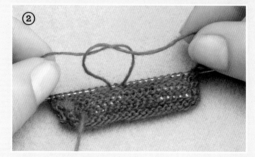

▲ If you've skipped a bead or strung a few in the wrong order, move the beads down the yarn and cut the yarn, leaving about a 4" tail. ① Add the missing bead, or remove the offending beads, and re-string them in the correct order. Begin knitting again with the "new" yarn, and after working two or three stitches, ② tie an overhand knot in the yarn ends to keep the beads from slipping off.

If you don't notice a mistake until you're done with the work, there is little hope of fixing it, but you can always try. If you have one bead of the wrong color placed in the work, you can break that bead out. I've done this by placing the end of a tapestry needle at the bead opening and tapping the other end with a hammer. This is risky business because you don't want to break the thread. Once you've successfully removed the offending bead, sew one into the empty spot, making sure you tip it in the proper direction, and weave both ends of the yarn into the back of the work.

Knitting Errors

▲ The most common mistake in bead knitting is allowing beads to fall to the back of the work. While knitting (or purling), be sure you're knitting above the bead in the previous row, using whatever extra fingers you have to keep that bead in position. ① If a bead falls to the back, you can usually stretch the work and ② use a knitting needle to pop it back into position on the right side.

Carpet Coasters

These coasters are done with the traditional pictorial bead knitting method, and I used the Eastern knit stitch (see page 24) on every other row. The charts were adapted from Frank Cooper's *Oriental Carpets in Miniature*. You could knit these without twisting every other row, but you'd have to use a fairly firm interfacing to force the resulting biased knitting into a square.

Finished Measurements	4¼" (11 cm) square
Yarn	DMC Size 8 perle cotton, .3 oz (10 g) / 87 yd (80 m); Red, 1 ball
Beads	Size 11° seed beads: 6 g green, 2 g white, 1 g each gold, red, and blue for Chart 1; and 6 g green, 2 g each gold and red, 1 g each white and blue for Chart 2
Needles	US 0000 (1.25 mm), *or size you need to obtain correct gauge*
Gauge	11 stitches = 1" (2.5 cm)
Other Supplies	Big eye beading needle, small tapestry needle, 4¼" (11 cm) square of felt for each coaster, sewing needle and coordinating sewing thread
Abbreviations	**KB** knit with bead (see page 25) **PB** purl with bead (see page 25)

Stringing the Beads

- Using a big eye beading needle, string beads row by row according to the chart for flat (back-and-forth) knitting (see pages 26–27).

Knitting the Coaster

- **SETUP (RS):** Cast on 49 stitches and purl 1 row without beads.
- **ROW 1:** K2, KB45, K2.
- **ROW 2:** P2, PB45, P2.
- Repeat Rows 1 and 2 until all beads have been knitted.
- Work 2 rows without beads.
- Bind off.
- Weave in ends using a tapestry needle.

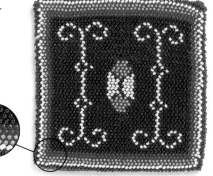

Finishing

- Hand sew beadwork to felt back with small stitches using a sewing needle and thread.

Notice how dramatically changing one bead color can affect the overall look of a design. In the top coaster, an opaque apricot bead was used for gold; in the bottom coaster, a transparent topaz bead was used for gold. While the transparent beads look gold in their container, they appear to change color when used with red thread.

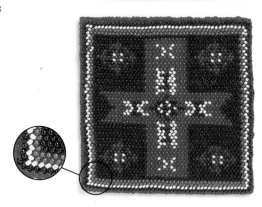

CHART 1

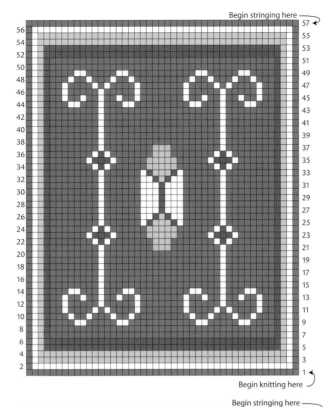

Begin stringing here → 57

Begin knitting here

CHART 2

Begin stringing here → 57

Begin knitting here

Turquoise Mixed Bag

This is a great project for practicing bead knitting since you don't have to follow a chart. You can mix as many colors as you want and vary the percentage of each color to get just the look you're after. There are also premixed color schemes available, such as the one used in this project that came from Caravan Beads (see page 154). I used the Eastern knit stitch (see page 24) on every other row.

Finished Measurements	6" (15 cm) wide × 4" (10 cm) tall plus 2½" (6.5 cm) flap
Yarn	J&P Coats Royale Classic Crochet Thread Size 10/350 yd (320 m); Black, 1 spool
Beads	Size 8° seed beads, mix of 6–7 coordinating colors, 75 g total
Needles	US 00 (1.75 mm), *or size you need to obtain the correct gauge*
Gauge	8 stitches = 1" (2.5 cm)
Other Supplies	Big eye beading needle, tapestry needle, 6" × 11" (15 cm × 28 cm) piece of fusible interfacing, 7" × 12" (18 cm × 30.5 cm) piece of lining fabric, sewing needle and coordinating sewing thread, 24" (61 cm) cord with tassels
Abbreviations	**KB** knit with bead (see page 25) **PB** purl with bead (see page 25)

● ● ALTERNATE DESIGN IDEA ● ●

Beads for a bag may be strung to produce a pattern like this checkerboard. This swatch is knitted in variegated purple crochet cotton with dark purple and lavender beads.

Stringing the Beads

- Mix all beads together to make a "bead soup." Using a big eye beading needle, string beads onto the yarn randomly.

Knitting the Bag

- **SETUP (RS):** Cast on 52 stitches. Purl 1 row without beads.
- **ROW 1:** K2, KB48, K2.
- **ROW 2:** P2, PB48, P2.
- Repeat Rows 1 and 2 until piece measures 11" (28 cm).
- Work 1 or 2 rows without beads.
- **BIND OFF.**
- Weave in ends using a tapestry needle.

Finishing

- Following manufacturer's instructions, fuse interfacing to lining.
- Hand sew lining to inside of beaded piece with small stitches using a sewing needle and thread.
- Fold bottom of bag up 4" (10 cm) with beaded side facing out and stitch side seams using a tapestry needle.
- Using a sewing needle and thread, stitch the ends of the cord to sides of flap, allowing tassels to hang from corners (see photo detail at right).

Colorful Diamonds Gloves

For these gloves, beads are knitted into some of the stitches, and the background is comprised of plain knit stitches. The gloves are knit in the round, and I used the Eastern knit stitch (see page 24) on every other round only in the beaded areas.

Finished Measurements	8" (20.5 cm) circumference, to fit medium woman's hand
Yarn	Rowan 4 Ply Soft, 100% merino wool, 1.75 oz (50 g) / 191 yd (175 m) *[Yarn band gauge: 28 stitches and 36 rows = 4" (10 cm) on US 3 (3.25 mm) needles]*; Color 1775 Navy, 2 balls
Beads	Size 8° seed beads: 228 pink (6 g); 228 blue (6 g); 104 lavender (3 g); 40 chartreuse (1 g)
Needles	Set of five US 3 (3.25 mm) double-pointed needles, *or size you need to obtain correct gauge*
Gauge	24 stitches = 4" (10 cm) in bead-knitted pattern
Other Supplies	Big eye beading needle, stitch markers, cotton string for holders, tapestry needle
Abbreviations	**KB** knit with bead (see page 25)

Stringing the Beads

- String beads for the motif using a big eye beading needle. Follow the chart on page 43 row by row from left to right, beginning at the upper left. For example:
- **ROUND 1:** 1 pink, 1 blue.
- **ROUND 2:** 3 pink, 3 blue.
- **ROUND 3:** 4 pink, 4 blue.
- **ROUND 4:** 2 pink, 1 green, 2 pink, 2 blue, 1 green, 2 blue.
- Continue until all beads on the chart are strung onto one ball of yarn.
- For the cuff, string *1 pink, 1 blue; repeat from * twenty-nine more times on the same ball of yarn, after the beads for the chart.
- Repeat with second ball of yarn for the other glove and set aside.

Knitting the Cuff

- **SETUP:** Cast on 50 stitches and divide onto four double-pointed needles as follows.

    Needles 1 and 3: 10 stitches each.

    Needles 2 and 4: 15 stitches each.

    Join into a round, being careful not to twist the stitches.
- **ROUNDS 1–3:** *K3, P2; repeat from *.
- **ROUND 4:** *K1, KB1, K1, P2; repeat from *.
- Repeat Rounds 1–4 five more times, then repeat Rounds 1–3 once more.

●● **ALTERNATE DESIGN IDEA** ●●

Changing the type of bead can yield a completely different look, such as this one that has a folk or ethnic feel to it. The swatch is knitted in 4 Ply Soft, color 373 Sooty, with orange, cream, green, and brown opaque beads.

Knitting the Hand

- **NEXT ROUND:** Knit, increasing 4 stitches evenly spaced. *You now have 54 stitches.*

    Rearrange the stitches as follows.

    Needles 1 and 3: 13 stitches each.

    Needles 2 and 4: 14 stitches each.

- Knit 2 rounds even.

Knitting the Thumb Gusset and Working the Chart

LEFT GLOVE

- **SETUP:** K23, place marker, K1, place marker, K3, K27 for the Back stitches.
- **ROUND 1:** Knit to marker, slip marker, M1, knit to next marker, M1, slip marker, K3; work Row 1 of chart over 27 Back stitches.
- **ROUND 2:** Knit all Palm stitches; work next row of chart over 27 Back stitches.
- **NEXT ROUNDS:** Repeat Rounds 1 and 2 until you have 17 stitches between markers for the Thumb Gusset.
- **NEXT ROUND:** Knit to marker, place 17 Thumb Gusset stitches on string to hold, cast on 1 stitch using the backward loop method (see page 150), rejoin, and K3. Work chart over 27 Back stitches. *You now have 54 stitches.*
- **NEXT ROUNDS:** Continue working Palm stitches even and working chart over Back stitches until chart is complete.
- Knit 4 rounds even.

RIGHT GLOVE

- **SETUP:** K27 stitches for the Back, K3, place marker, K1, place marker, K23 Palm stitches.

(continued on next page)

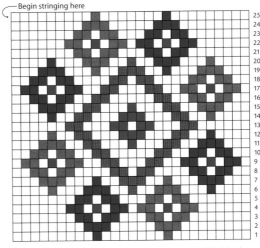

Begin stringing here

25
24
23
22
21
20
19
18
17
16
15
14
13
12
11
10
9
8
7
6
5
4
3
2
1

Begin knitting here

- **ROUND 1:** Work Row 1 of chart over 27 Back stitches, knit to marker, slip marker, M1, knit to next marker, M1, K23 Palm stitches.
- **ROUND 2:** Work next row of chart over 27 Back stitches, knit all Palm stitches.
- **NEXT ROUNDS:** Repeat Rounds 1 and 2 until you have 17 stitches between the markers for the Thumb Gusset.
- **NEXT ROUND:** Work chart over 27 Back stitches, knit to marker, place 17 thumb gusset stitches on string to hold, cast on 1 stitch using the backward loop method (see page 150), rejoin, and K23. *You now have* 54 stitches.
- **NEXT ROUNDS:** Continue working chart over Back stitches and working Palm stitches even until chart is complete.
- Knit 4 rounds even.

Knitting the Little Finger

BOTH GLOVES
- **SETUP:** K7, place following 40 stitches on string to hold. Cast on 4 stitches using the backward loop method and knit remaining 7 stitches. *You now have* 18 stitches. Arrange stitches onto three double-pointed needles.
- **NEXT ROUNDS:** Knit even on 18 stitches until finger measures 2" (5 cm), or ¼" (6 mm) from desired finished length.
- **ROUND 1:** *K2, K2tog; repeat from *, end K2. *You now have* 14 stitches.
- **ROUND 2:** Knit.
- **ROUND 3:** *K1, K2tog; repeat from *, end K2. *You now have* 10 stitches.
- **ROUND 4:** *K2tog; repeat from *. *You now have* 5 stitches.
Note: Adjust stitches on needles as necessary to work the decreases.
- Cut yarn, leaving an 8" (20 cm) tail.
- Thread tail onto tapestry needle and draw through remaining 5 stitches twice. Pass tail to inside, tie off securely, and weave in end.

Continuing the Hand
- **SETUP:** Place 40 stitches from string holder onto four double-pointed needles.

LEFT GLOVE

- **ROUND 1:** Attach yarn at palm side of Little Finger, K40, pick up and knit (see page 152) 6 stitches over the 4 cast-on stitches of the Little Finger (pick up 1, knit 1 into each of the 4 cast-on stitches, pick up 1). Join into a round.
- **ROUND 2:** K40, slip 1, K1, psso, K2, K2tog. *You now have* 44 stitches.
- **ROUNDS 3–5:** Knit 3 rounds even.

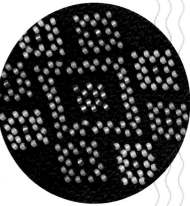

RIGHT GLOVE

- **ROUND 1:** Attach yarn at palm side of Little Finger, pick up and knit 6 stitches over 4 cast-on stitches as for Left Glove, and K40. Join into a round.
- **ROUND 2:** Slip 1, K1, psso, K2, K2tog, K40. *You now have* 44 stitches.
- **ROUNDS 3–5:** Knit 3 rounds even.

Knitting the Ring Finger

BOTH GLOVES

- **SETUP:** Knit 6, place following 28 stitches on string to hold. Cast on 4 and knit remaining 10 stitches. *You now have* 20 stitches. Arrange stitches onto three double-pointed needles.
- **NEXT ROUNDS:** Knit even on 20 stitches until finger measures 2½" (6.5 cm), or ¼" (6 mm) from desired finished length.
- **ROUND 1:** *K2, K2tog; repeat from *. *You now have* 15 stitches.
- **ROUND 2:** Knit.
- **ROUND 3:** *K1, K2tog; repeat from *. *You now have* 10 stitches.
- **ROUND 4:** *K2tog; repeat from *. *You now have* 5 stitches.
- Cut yarn, leaving an 8" (20 cm) tail.
- Thread tail onto tapestry needle and draw through remaining 5 stitches twice. Pass tail to inside, tie off securely, and weave in end.

Knitting the Middle Finger

LEFT GLOVE

- **SETUP:** Attach yarn at palm side of Ring Finger, knit first 6 held stitches, cast on 4, leave the next 16 stitches on the holder and knit the last 6 held stitches, pick up and knit 6 stitches over the 4 cast-on stitches of the Ring Finger (pick up 1, knit 1 into each of the 4 cast-on stitches, pick up 1). *You now have* 22 stitches. Arrange stitches onto three double-pointed needles and join into a round.
- **NEXT ROUND:** K16, slip 1, K1, psso, K2, K2tog. *You now have* 20 stitches.
- Knit even until finger measures 2¾" (7 cm), or ¼" (6 mm) from desired finished length.
- Complete as for Ring Finger.

RIGHT GLOVE

- **SETUP:** Attach yarn at palm side of Ring Finger, pick up and knit 6 stitches over the 4 cast-on stitches of the Ring Finger, knit first 6 held stitches, cast on 4, leave the next 16 stitches on the holder and knit last 6 held stitches. *You now have* 22 stitches. Arrange stitches onto three double-pointed needles and join into a round.
- **NEXT ROUND:** Slip 1, K1, psso, K2, K2tog, K16. *You now have* 20 stitches.
- Proceed as for Left Glove.

Knitting the Index Finger

LEFT GLOVE

- **SETUP:** Attach yarn at palm side of Middle Finger, knit remaining 16 stitches from holder, pick up and knit 6 stitches over the 4 cast-on stitches of the Middle Finger (pick up 1, knit 1 into each of the 4 cast-on stitches, pick up 1). Arrange stitches onto three double-pointed needles and join into a round.
- Proceed and complete as for Ring Finger.

RIGHT GLOVE

- **SETUP:** Attach yarn at palm side of Middle Finger, pick up and knit 6 stitches over the 4 cast-on stitches of the Middle Finger as for Left Glove, and knit remaining 16 stitches from holder. Arrange stitches onto three double-pointed needles and join into a round.
- Proceed as for Left Glove.

Knitting the Thumb

LEFT GLOVE

- **SETUP:** Place 17 held Thumb stitches onto two double-pointed needles. Attach yarn at palm side of Thumb Gusset and K17. Pick up 4 stitches, including the 1 cast-on stitch. *You now have* 21 stitches.
- **NEXT ROUNDS:** Knit even on these 21 stitches until thumb measures 1¾" (4.5 cm), or ¼" (6 mm) less than desired finished length.
- **ROUND 1:** *K2, K2tog; repeat from * to last stitch, K1. *You now have* 16 stitches.
- **ROUND 2:** Knit.
- **ROUND 3:** *K1, K2tog; repeat from * to last stitch, K1. *You now have* 11 stitches.
- **ROUND 4:** *K2tog; repeat from * to last stitch, K1. *You now have* 6 stitches.
- Finish as for the other fingers.

RIGHT GLOVE

- **SETUP:** Place 17 held Thumb stitches onto two double-pointed needles. Attach yarn at palm side of Thumb Gusset and pick up 4 stitches, including the 1 cast-on stitch, K17.
- Proceed as for Left Glove.

Finishing

- Weave in all ends with a tapestry needle, using tails to close up any holes that may have formed at the base of fingers or thumbs.

③ Beaded Knitting

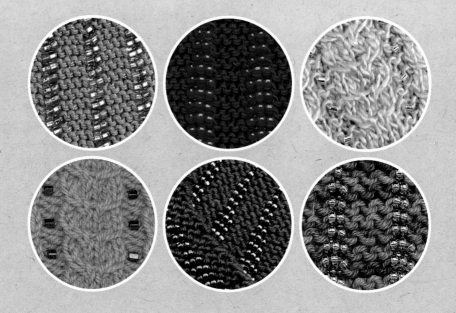

With beaded knitting, a bead (or beads) lies on the thread between two stitches. This technique experienced a revival during the 1990s, when many people knitted little amulet bags to be worn around the neck. The beads may be all one color, or you may mix the colors for different effects. Varying the number of beads that lie between two stitches will shape the knitted piece, as in the Golden Purse (see page 58) and the ends of the Iridescent Beaded Scarf (see page 54). Using only one bead between the stitches can create an allover glow, as in the Crystal Cardigan (see page 64).

Beads lying between two knit stitches show on the back of the work; beads lying between two purl stitches show on the front of the work. Working in garter stitch allows beads to be incorporated on both sides of the fabric; this is how the shaped pieces are done.

Beaded knitting requires that you pre-string the beads, and they may be slightly larger or smaller than a knit stitch.

BEADING BETWEEN KNIT STITCHES

▲ Knit to the place where you want the bead, slide the bead right up against the needle, and knit the next stitch. The bead will show on the side of the fabric facing away from you. If you place a bead in this manner from the wrong side of the knitting, the bead will show on the front. This technique is used in the Crystal Cardigan (see page 64).

BEADING BETWEEN PURL STITCHES

▲ Purl to the place where you want the bead, slide the bead right up against the needle, and purl the next stitch. The bead will show on the side of the fabric facing you.

If your pattern calls for knit stitches, knit to the stitch before the bead, purl one stitch, slide the bead right up against the needle, purl the next stitch, and continue in your pattern as established. This technique allows you to place a bead on the right side of the fabric while working a right-side row.

BEADING WITH GARTER AND REVERSE STOCKINETTE STITCHES

When working in garter stitch, whether the garter stitch is allover as in the Golden Purse (see page 58) or only in certain areas as in the body of the Iridescent Beaded Scarf (see page 54), you can place beads on both sides of the work. Proceed as outlined earlier in Beading between Knit Stitches, placing beads on both right- and wrong-side rows.

When knitting an allover garter stitch piece, beads can be placed anywhere. Place beads on wrong-side rows, and they'll show on the right side.

Here beads are placed on a reverse stockinette stitch ground between cables. The beads are placed between purl stitches on right-side rows.

SHAPING WITH BEADS

Increasing the number of beads between stitches will push the knitting outward and add width to the piece. Decreasing the number of beads will bring the width back in.

You can shape the knitted fabric by increasing and decreasing the number of beads between the stitches. Beads are placed between knit stitches on both right- and wrong-side rows.

CASTING ON AND BINDING OFF WITH MULTIPLE BEADS

The Iridescent Beaded Scarf (see page 54) was started at the center back and worked down to each end. Then the stitches were bound off. You could also begin at the ends and finish at the center back, or you could cast on at one end and bind off at the other.

Casting On

▲ ① To cast on, begin with a slip knot on the needle.

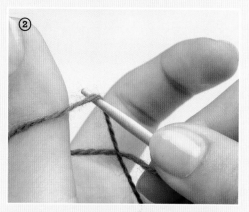

▲ ② Use the backward loop method (see page 150) to cast on the required number of stitches.

▲ ③ Slide beads up against the needle and cast on more stitches with the backward loop method.

Binding Off

When you're ready to bind off, cut the yarn, leaving a long tail.

string beads on tail

▲ Bind off stitches to the first bead, pulling the tail all the way through the last stitch. String the required number of beads on the tail, slide them up, and bind off stitches to the next bead, pulling the tail all the way through the last stitch. Repeat to end of row.

CORRECTING MISTAKES

Yes, mistakes happen. As with most knitting mistakes, ripping back and re-knitting is the best cure. Still, there are a couple of other possibilities.

▲ **Missed single bead.** If you inadvertently missed a bead when working one bead at a time, use a tapestry needle to anchor a piece of yarn in the knitting so it exits the stitch next to where the bead is missing.

Remove the tapestry needle, string on a bead, and replace the tapestry needle. ① Pass through the next stitch, leaving the bead between the stitches. ② Weave in the tails.

▲ **Missed multiple bead.** If you missed a bead when working with multiples, use a tapestry needle to anchor a piece of yarn in the knitting so it exits the stitch next to the strand holding too few beads.

① Remove the tapestry needle, thread the yarn onto a big eye beading needle, and string a bead.

② Slide the bead up against the knitting and pass through all beads on the strand.

③ Replace the tapestry needle and weave in the tails.

Note: This correction will work only if there is enough room inside the beads for a second pass of a doubled yarn. If the hole is too small to accommodate the second pass, you could try stringing the missing bead onto a thinner yarn and proceeding as outlined above.

Iridescent Beaded Scarf

This scarf has a drop stitch pattern with beaded garter rows between. The ends are shaped by gradually increasing from one to five beads between the stitches. Although this one is knitted from the center back to the ends, you also could begin or end with the scalloped ends (see page 52 for casting on and binding off with beads).

Finished Measurements	4" (10 cm) wide × 58" (147.5 cm) long
Yarn	Knit One, Crochet Too Ambrosia, 70% baby alpaca/20% silk/10% cashmere, 1.75 oz (50 g)/137 yd (125 m) *[Yarn band gauge: 24 stitches = 4" (10 cm) on US 3 (3.25 mm) needles]*; Color 688 French Blue, 2 skeins
Beads	Size 8° metallic green iris seed beads, 75 g
Needles	US 3 (3.25 mm) straight needles, *or size you need to obtain correct gauge*
Gauge	20 stitches = 4" (10 cm)
Other Supplies	Big eye beading needle, scrap yarn for provisional cast-on, tapestry needle
Abbreviations	**S1B** slide 1 bead up against needle (S2B=slide 2 beads, etc.) (see page 50)

Stringing the Beads

• String half the beads onto 1 skein of yarn. There are approximately 10 beads to the inch (2.5 cm), so you should have about 7 yards (6.5 m) of beads on the yarn. Repeat with the second skein.

• • **ALTERNATE DESIGN IDEA** • •

Beads are less visible when used on a variegated yarn than on a solid, but they'll sparkle just as much. The swatch is knitted in Handpainted Ambrosia, color 1480 Tourmaline, with smoky amethyst beads.

Knitting the First Half of the Scarf

- SETUP: Using a provisional method (see page 152), cast on 21 stitches.
- ROW 1: *K3, S1B; repeat from * to last 3 stitches, K3.
- ROW 2: Repeat Row 1.
- ROW 3: *K1, yo; repeat from * to last stitch, K1.
- ROW 4: Knit, dropping yos.
- Repeat Rows 1–4 sixty-five times or until piece measures 24" (61 cm).

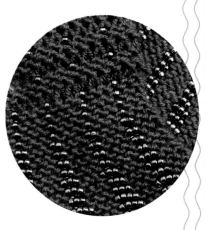

Knitting the Scarf End

- ROWS 1–8: *K3, S1B; repeat from * to last 3 stitches, K3.
- ROWS 9–16: *K3, S2B; repeat from * to last 3 stitches, K3.
- ROWS 17–22: *K3, S3B; repeat from * to last 3 stitches, K3.
- ROWS 23–28: *K3, S4B; repeat from * to last 3 stitches, K3.
- ROWS 29–33: *K3, S5B; repeat from * to last 3 stitches, K3.
- ROW 34: Cut yarn, leaving a 10" (25 cm) tail. Remove any beads from the tail. Bind off 3 stitches, pulling the tail through the last stitch. *Thread 5 beads onto tail, slide up snug, and bind off 3 stitches, pulling the tail through the last stitch; repeat from *.

Knitting the Second Half of the Scarf

- Remove the provisional cast-on and place 21 stitches on needle.
- Beginning with Row 3 of pattern and on the opposite side from the cast-on tail, knit the second half of the scarf to match the first.
- Weave in ends using a tapestry needle.

Golden Purse

Can't you just see this purse with a flapper's dress? Now picture it with basic black — or with jeans. Anything goes! The hardware that keeps the purse open and closed is hidden inside a casing, and the chain is attached with jump rings.

Finished Measurements	8" (20.5 cm) at widest point × 6" (15 cm) tall
Yarn	J&P Coats Royale Metallic Crochet Thread Size 10, 88% mercerized cotton/12% metallic, 100 yd (91 m); Color 0090G Gold, 3 spools
Beads	Size 6° silver-lined gold seed beads, 150 g
Needles	US 3 (3.25 mm) straight needles
Other Supplies	Big eye beading needle, tapestry needle that fits through beads, 6" (15 cm) straight hex-open purse frame, 40" (102 cm) medium chain with 2 jump rings
Abbreviations	**S1B** slide 1 bead up against needle (S2B=slide 2 beads, etc.) (see page 50)

Note: Yarn is used doubled throughout.

● ● **ALTERNATE DESIGN IDEA** ● ●

Transparent beads reflect less light than the silver-lined ones in the golden purse, but the fiery red is equally brilliant. The swatch is knitted in dark red crochet cotton with transparent ruby red beads.

Preparing the Yarn

- Wind two spools of yarn together (doubled) into one ball. Thread 135 g of the beads onto this doubled yarn. You will have approximately 6.5 yards (6 m) of strung beads.

Knitting the Frame Casing

Note: This yarn tends to bias in stockinette stitch, but you can correct this by knitting through the back loop on right-side rows and purling as usual on wrong-side rows.

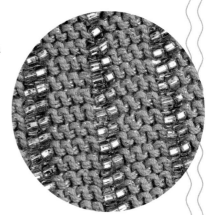

- **SETUP:** Cast on 38 stitches.
- **NEXT ROWS:** Work stockinette stitch for ¾" (2 cm).
- **NEXT ROW:** If you end on a wrong-side row, purl the next row. If you end on a right-side row, knit the next row. This creates a turning ridge on the right side.
- **NEXT ROWS:** Work stockinette stitch for another ¾" (2 cm).

Knitting and Beading the Bag

- **NEXT ROWS:** Keeping the first and last stitches as stockinette edge stitches and working garter stitch in between, bead knit as follows.
- **RIGHT-SIDE ROWS 1–11:** K3, S1B, *K4, S1B; repeat from * to last 3 stitches, K3.
- **WRONG-SIDE ROWS 2–12:** P1, K2, S1B, *K4, S1B; repeat from * to last 3 stitches, K2, P1.
- **RIGHT-SIDE ROWS 13–35:** K3, S2B, *K4, S2B; repeat from * to last 3 stitches, K3.
- **WRONG-SIDE ROWS 14–36:** P1, K2, S2B, *K4, S2B; repeat from * to last 3 stitches, K2, P1.
- **RIGHT-SIDE ROWS 37–83:** K3, S3B, *K4, S3B; repeat from * to last 3 stitches, K3.
- **WRONG-SIDE ROWS 38–84:** P1, K2, S3B, *K4, S3B; repeat from * to last 3 stitches, K2, P1.
- **RIGHT-SIDE ROWS 85–107:** K3, S2B, *K4, S2B; repeat from * to last 3 stitches, K3.

(continued on next page)

- **WRONG-SIDE ROWS 86–108:** P1, K2, S2B, *K4, S2B; repeat from * to last 3 stitches, K2, P1.
- **RIGHT-SIDE ROWS 109–119:** K3, S1B, *K4, S1B; repeat from * to last 3 stitches, K3.
- **WRONG-SIDE ROWS 110–120:** P1, K2, S1B, *K4, S1B; repeat from * to last 3 stitches, K2, P1.
- Remove any leftover beads from the yarn. If you still have yarn, you may continue. If you are near the end of the yarn, measure 32 yards (29.5 m) and wind it into a doubled ball.
- **NEXT ROWS:** Work stockinette stitch for ¾" (2 cm).
- **NEXT ROW:** If you end on a wrong-side row, purl the next row. If you end on a right-side row, knit the next row. This creates a turning ridge on the right side.
- **NEXT ROWS:** Work stockinette stitch for another ¾" (2 cm). Bind off loosely.

Finishing

- Sew the side seams using a tapestry needle.
- Place the hex-open frame inside the bag, fold the casing over the frame along the turning ridge, and stitch the casing in place with a tapestry needle and crochet thread (I used a nearly invisible back-stitch; see page 150).
- Attach the chain to the jump rings and sew the rings to the inside bottom of the casing at each side.
- Weave in ends with a tapestry needle.

Adding the Bead Fringe

Note: The fringe is added with a backstitch (see page 150).

- Thread a tapestry needle with 3 yards (3 m) of yarn and anchor the yarn in a stitch in the bottom row of the casing.
- *Pick up five beads, insert needle 2 stitches to the right, bring needle out 4 stitches to the left of where it went in; repeat from * along entire bottom row of the casing, front and back. Repeat three more times above this first row.

Crystal Cardigan

This yarn is lovely for beading; the subtle sheen of the silk is a perfect complement to the sparkling lined beads. Designed with shaping at the waist and a cropped length, this cardigan sweater is classic and contemporary at the same time.

Finished Measurements	38" (42", 46") (96.5 cm [106.5 cm, 117 cm]) chest circumference
Yarn	Debbie Bliss Pure Silk, 100% silk, 1.75 oz (50 g) / 132 yd (125 m) *[Yarn band gauge: 24 stitches and 32 rows = 4" (10 cm) on US 6 (4 mm) needles]*; Color 27002 Pearl Gray, 10 (11, 12) skeins
Beads	Size 8° silver-lined crystal cylinder beads, 100 g
Needles	US 6 (4 mm) circular needle 32" (80 cm) long plus extra needle for three-needle bind-off, *or size you need to obtain the correct gauge*
Gauge	31 stitches and 40 rows = 4" (10 cm) in pattern
Other Supplies	Big eye beading needle, cable needle, scrap yarn for holders, tapestry needle, eight size 3 hooks and bars, tapestry needle that will fit through loops of hooks and bars
Abbreviations	**C2L** slip 1 stitch onto cable needle and hold in front, K1 from left needle, K1 from cable needle **C2R** slip 1 stitch onto cable needle and hold in back, K1 from left needle, K1 from cable needle **C3L** slip 1 stitch onto cable needle and hold in front, K2 from left needle, K1 from cable needle **C3R** slip 2 stitches onto cable needle and hold in back, K1 from left needle, K2 from cable needle **DC** decrease cable: slip 2 stitches onto cable needle and hold in back, K1 from left needle, K2tog tbl from cable needle; slip 1 stitch onto cable needle and hold in front, K2tog from left needle, K1 from cable needle **IC** increase cable: slip 1 stitch onto cable needle and hold in back, K1 from left needle, Kfb from cable needle; slip 1 stitch onto cable needle and hold in front, Kfb from left needle, K1 from cable needle **S1B** slide 1 bead up against the needle (see page 50)

● ● ALTERNATE DESIGN IDEA ● ●

Cut beads reflect light from more than one surface, making a woolen-blend yarn come alive. The swatch is knitted in Classic Elite Fresco (wool/baby alpaca/angora), color 5367 Blue Turquoise, with 6° dark turquoise iridescent hex-cut beads.

·· BEADS AND CABLE ··	STITCH PATTERN

ROW 1 (RS): Slip 1 (edge stitch) *P2, K6; repeat from * to last 3 stitches, P2, K1 (edge stitch).

ROW 2: Slip 1 (edge stitch), *K2, P6; repeat from * to last 3 stitches, K2, P1 (edge stitch).

ROW 3: Slip 1 (edge stitch), *P2, C3R, C3L; repeat from * to last 3 stitches, P2, K1 (edge stitch).

ROW 4: Slip 1 (edge stitch) *K1, SB, K1, P6; repeat from * to last 3 stitches, K1, SB, K1, P1 (edge stitch).

Repeat Rows 1–4 for pattern.

S 38"   **M** 42"   **L** 46"

Preparing the Yarn

Note: If you're working with Pure Silk, wind your skeins by hand. The yarn will twist like mad if you try using a ball winder, and you could spend hours untangling the resulting beaded mess.

• String about 272 beads (28" [71 cm]) onto each ball of yarn.

Knitting the Lower Body

Note: The lower body is worked in one piece up to the armholes, and then the fronts and back are worked separately to the shoulders. The waist is tapered by reducing some of the 6-stitch cables to 4-stitch cables and then increasing them back to their original size.

• **SETUP:** Cast on   **S** 292 sts   **M** 324 sts   **L** 356 sts

• **NEXT ROWS:** Work Beads and Cable stitch pattern until measurement from cast-on edge is

          S 2" (5 cm)   **M** 2½" (6.5 cm)   **L** 3" (7.5 cm)

• End with Row 2 of pattern.

Shaping the Waist

• Begin waist shaping by decreasing ten of the 6-stitch cables to 4-stitch cables as follows.

• **DECREASE ROW 1 (ROW 3 OF PATTERN):**

In pattern as established, work   **S** 11 sts   **M** 11 sts   **L** 19 sts

DC next and then every following fourth cable four times.

Work even   **S** 0 cables   **M** 4 cables   **L** 6 cables

DC next and then every following fourth cable four times.

In pattern as established, work the remaining

          S 11 sts   **M** 11 sts   **L** 19 sts

You now have   **S** 272 sts   **M** 304 sts   **L** 336 sts

(continued on next page)

	S 38"	**M** 42"	**L** 46"

- **NEXT ROW:** Work Row 4 in newly established pattern (P4 instead of P6 on reduced cables).
- **NEXT ROWS:** Continue in pattern as established, but work 4-stitch cables with C2R and C2L, until you have completed two more 4-row cable repeats.
- **NEXT 2 ROWS:** Work Rows 1 and 2 of pattern.
- **DECREASE ROW 2 (ROW 3 OF PATTERN):**

  In pattern as established, work to

	S 4th cable	**M** 4th cable	**L** 5th cable

  DC this and then every following fourth cable

	S 3 times	**M** 4 times	**L** 4 times

  Work even the next

	S 4 cables	**M** 0 cables	**L** 2 cables

  DC next and then every following fourth cable

	S 3 times	**M** 4 times	**L** 4 times

  Work even in pattern to end of row.

  You now have

	S 256 sts	**M** 284 sts	**L** 316 sts

- **NEXT ROWS:** Continue even in pattern until you have completed three more 4-row cable repeats, ending on Row 2 of pattern.
- **INCREASE ROW 1 (ROW 3 OF PATTERN):**

  In pattern as established, work to

	S 4th cable	**M** 4th cable	**L** 5th cable

  IC this and then every following fourth cable

	S 3 times	**M** 4 times	**L** 4 times

  Work without increasing the next

	S 4 cables	**M** 0 cables	**L** 2 cables

  IC next and then every following fourth cable

	S 3 times	**M** 4 times	**L** 4 times

  Work even in pattern to end of row.

  You now have

	S 272 sts	**M** 304 sts	**L** 336 sts

- **NEXT ROW:** Work Row 4 in newly established pattern (returning to P6 instead of P4 on increased cables).
- **NEXT 8 ROWS:** Continue in pattern as established until you have completed two more 4-row cable repeats.
- **NEXT ROWS:** Work Rows 1 and 2.
- **INCREASE ROW 2 (ROW 3 OF PATTERN):**

  In pattern as established, work

	S 11 sts	**M** 11 sts	**L** 19 sts

  IC next and then every following fourth cable four times.

  Work without increasing the next

	S 0 cables	**M** 4 cables	**L** 6 cables

	S 38"	**M** 42"	**L** 46"

IC next and then every following fourth cable four times.

In pattern as established, work the last

	S 11 sts	**M** 11 sts	**L** 19 sts

You now have

	S 292 sts	**M** 324 sts	**L** 356 sts

• **NEXT ROWS:** Work even in pattern as established until piece measures

	S 8½" (21.5 cm)	**M** 9½" (24 cm)	**L** 10½" (26.5 cm)

• End with Row 4 of pattern.

Dividing for Fronts and Back

• **NEXT ROW (RS):**

For the Right Front, work in pattern as established and then place on a holder

	S 60 sts	**M** 68 sts	**L** 76 sts

Bind off next 28 stitches for Right Underarm.

In pattern as established for Back, work the next

	S 116 sts	**M** 132 sts	**L** 148 sts

Place on holder for Left Front and Underarm the remaining

	S 88 sts	**M** 96 sts	**L** 104 sts

Knitting the Back

• **NEXT ROW:** On Back stitches only, work Row 2 of pattern over

	S 116 sts	**M** 132 sts	**L** 148 sts

• **DECREASE ROW (RS):** K1 (edge stitch), slip 1, K1, psso, work even in pattern to last 3 stitches, K2tog, K1 (edge stitch).

• **NEXT ROWS:** Continue in pattern as established, keeping first and last edge stitches in stockinette stitch, and repeat decrease row every right-side row seven more times.

You now have

	S 100 sts	**M** 116 sts	**L** 132 sts

• **NEXT ROWS:** Work even in pattern as established until measurement from underarm bind-off is

	S 8" (20.5 cm)	**M** 8½" (21.5 cm)	**L** 9" (23 cm)

• End with Row 4 of pattern.

• **NEXT ROW:**

For Right Shoulder, work in pattern and place on holder the first

	S 27 sts	**M** 33 sts	**L** 39 sts

For Back Neck, bind off

	S 46 sts	**M** 50 sts	**L** 54 sts

For Left Shoulder, work in pattern and place on holder the remaining

	S 27 sts	**M** 33 sts	**L** 39 sts

	🅢 38"	🅜 42"	🅛 46"

Knitting the Right Front

- **SETUP:** Return to needle from holder for Right Front

	🅢 60 sts	🅜 68 sts	🅛 76 sts

- **NEXT ROW:** With wrong side facing, join yarn and work Row 2 of pattern.
- **DECREASE ROW (RS):** Slip 1 (edge stitch), K1, slip 1, K1, psso (neck decrease), work in pattern to last 3 stitches, K2tog (armhole decrease), K1 (edge stitch).
- **NEXT ROWS:** Continue in pattern as established and repeat decrease row every right-side row seven more times. *You now have*

	🅢 44 sts	🅜 52 sts	🅛 60 sts

- **NEXT ROWS:** Continue in pattern as established and work neck decrease only on every right-side row

	🅢 10 times	🅜 12 times	🅛 14 times
You now have	🅢 34 sts	🅜 40 sts	🅛 46 sts

- **NEXT ROWS:** Continue in pattern as established and work neck decrease every other right-side row (every 4th row) seven times.

	🅢 27 sts	🅜 33 sts	🅛 39 sts
You now have			

- **NEXT ROWS:** Continue in pattern as established until Right Front matches Back, ending with Row 4 of pattern. Place Right Front shoulder stitches on a holder.

Knitting the Left Front

- **SETUP:** Return to needle from holder for Left Front

	🅢 88 sts	🅜 96 sts	🅛 104 sts

- **NEXT ROW:** With right side facing, join yarn, bind off 28 stitches for Left Underarm, and work Row 2 of pattern on remaining

	🅢 60 sts	🅜 68 sts	🅛 76 sts

- **DECREASE ROW (RS):** K1 (edge stitch), slip 1, K1, psso (armhole decrease), work in pattern as established to last 4 stitches, K2tog (neck decrease), K2.
- **NEXT ROWS:** Continue in pattern as established, remembering to slip the first stitch of every wrong-side row, and repeat decrease row every right-side row seven more times.

You now have	🅢 44 sts	🅜 52 sts	🅛 60 sts

- **NEXT ROWS:** Continue in pattern as established and work neck decrease only on every right-side row

	🅢 10 times	🅜 12 times	🅛 14 times
You now have	🅢 34 sts	🅜 40 sts	🅛 46 sts

- **NEXT ROWS:** Continue in pattern as established and work neck decrease every other right-side row (every 4th row) seven times.

You now have	🅢 27 sts	🅜 33 sts	🅛 39 sts

S 38"   **M** 42"   **L** 46"

- **NEXT ROWS:** Continue in pattern as established until Left Front matches Back, ending with Row 4 of pattern. Place Left Front shoulder stitches on a holder.

Knitting the Sleeves

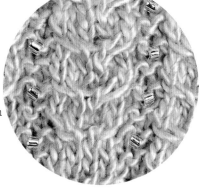

Notes: The sleeves are tapered like the waist by reducing 6-stitch cables to 4-stitch cables and then increasing them back to their original size, but the sleeve has only one decrease row. Maintain 3 edge stitches on both sides of the sleeves throughout, beginning and ending each right-side row with K3, beginning each wrong-side row as P1, K2, and ending each wrong-side row as K2, P1, adding beads as indicated for pattern stitch.

- **SETUP:** Cast on 68 stitches for all sizes.
- **ROWS 1–10:** Work Beads and Cable pattern Rows 1–4 twice, maintaining edge stitches as outlined above, and then work Rows 1 and 2.
- **DECREASE ROW (ROW 3 OF PATTERN):** Work in pattern as established and DC on all cables. *You now have* 52 stitches.
- **NEXT ROWS:** Continue even in pattern until you have completed one more 4-row cable repeat, ending on Row 2 of pattern.
- **INCREASE ROW (ROW 3 OF PATTERN):** Work in pattern as established and IC on all cables. *You now have* 68 stitches.
- **NEXT ROW:** Work Row 4 of pattern as established.

Beginning Sleeve Shaping

Note: Increase after the first 3 stitches and before the last 3 stitches on increase rows. Always increase on Row 1 of pattern.

- **NEXT ROWS:** Maintaining 3 edge stitches at the beginning and end of every row and continuing in pattern as established, increase 1 stitch at the beginning and end of every

4th row	**S** 14 times	**M** 16 times	**L** 18 times
You now have	**S** 96 sts	**M** 100 sts	**L** 104 sts

- **NEXT ROWS:** Maintaining 3 edge stitches at the beginning and end of every row and continuing in pattern as established, increase 1 stitch at the beginning and end of every

8th row	**S** 6 times	**M** 8 times	**L** 10 times
You now have	**S** 108 sts	**M** 116 sts	**L** 124 sts

(continued on next page)

(S) 38"   (M) 42"   (L) 46"

- **NEXT ROWS:** Work even in pattern as established until sleeve measures desired length from beginning, or   (S) 15" (38 cm)   (M) 16" (40.5 cm)   (L) 17" (43 cm)
- End with Row 4 of pattern.

Shaping the Sleeve Cap

Note: Maintain 1 edge stitch in stockinette stitch at the beginning and end of every row.

- **NEXT ROWS:** Bind off 14 stitches at the beginning of the next 2 rows. *You now have*

  (S) 80 sts   (M) 88 sts   (L) 96 sts

- **DECREASE ROW 1:** K1 (edge stitch) slip 1, K2tog, psso, work in pattern to last 4 stitches, K3tog, K1.
- **NEXT ROW:** Work even in established pattern.
- **NEXT ROWS:** Repeat these last 2 rows four more times. *You now have*

  (S) 60 sts   (M) 68 sts   (L) 76 sts

- **DECREASE ROW 2:** K1 (edge stitch), slip 1, K1, psso, work in pattern to last 3 stitches, K2tog, K1.
- **NEXT ROW:** Work even in established pattern.
- **NEXT ROWS:** Repeat these last 2 rows six more times. *You now have*

  (S) 46 sts   (M) 54 sts   (L) 62 sts

- **NEXT 3 ROWS:** Work 3 rows even.
- **NEXT ROW:** Work Decrease Row 2.
- Repeat these last 4 rows   (S) 3 more times   (M) 4 more times   (L) 5 more times

  You now have   (S) 38 sts   (M) 44 sts   (L) 50 sts

- **NEXT 2 ROWS:** Work 1 row even, then work Decrease Row 1.
- **NEXT 8 ROWS:** Repeat these last 2 rows four more times. *You now have*

  (S) 18 sts   (M) 24 sts   (L) 30 sts

- Bind off.

S 38"   **M** 42"   **L** 46"

Joining the Shoulders

- SETUP: Return to separate needles from holders the Front and Back Shoulder

  S 27 sts   **M** 33 sts   **L** 39 sts

- Working one side at a time, join the Front and Back Shoulder stitches together with the three-needle bind-off (see page 153).

Attaching the Sleeves

- Sew sleeve seams from cuffs to underarms with tapestry needle and yarn. Beginning at underarm seam, sew sleeves into armholes.

Finishing

- Using a tapestry needle threaded with about 24" (61 cm) of yarn, sew eight hooks to inside of Right Front edge as follows:
- Place one hook at the start of the neck shaping.
- From the bottom of the sweater, place one hook

  S 2" (5 cm)   **M** 2½" (6.5 cm)   **L** 3" (7.5 cm)

- Space six more hooks evenly between these two.
- Sew bars to the inside of the Left Front edge, opposite the hooks so the center fronts meet when closed. Weave in ends.

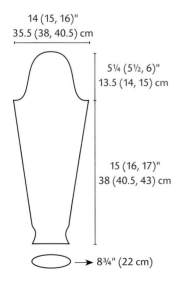

14 (15, 16)"
35.5 (38, 40.5) cm

5¼ (5½, 6)"
13.5 (14, 15) cm

15 (16, 17)"
38 (40.5, 43) cm

8¾" (22 cm)

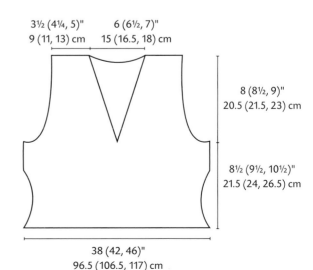

3½ (4¼, 5)"   6 (6½, 7)"
9 (11, 13) cm   15 (16.5, 18) cm

8 (8½, 9)"
20.5 (21.5, 23) cm

8½ (9½, 10½)"
21.5 (24, 26.5) cm

38 (42, 46)"
96.5 (106.5, 117) cm

④ Slipstitch Bead Knitting

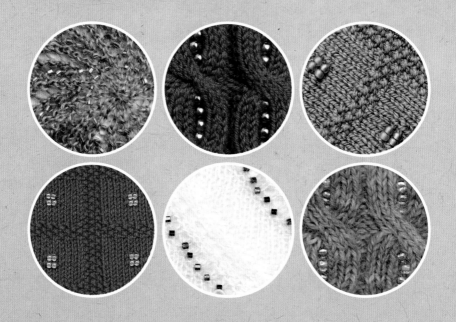

I was introduced to slipstitch bead knitting while
working on the Summer 1997 issue of *Interweave Knits*.
Michelle Poulin-Alfeld wrote an article for that issue about a
technique she'd developed called "embossed" bead knitting.
To "emboss" knitted fabric with beads, a bead is left lying
on a strand of yarn on top of a slipped stitch. Michelle's
method calls for surrounding the bead with purl stitches,
but I often use it on a stockinette stitch ground, as in the
Beads-Go-Sporty Pullover (see page 88), with cables as in
the Beady-Eyed Cable Socks (see page 82), or with any other
pattern, such as in the Magic Mohair Beret (see page 78).

Because you're working over slipped stitches, you can
work beads at the same place only on every other row.
You may place beads on the right side while working
from either side of the knitting. Slipstitch bead knitting
requires pre-stringing beads, and one bead should be
close in size to one stitch.

SLIPSTITCHING A SINGLE BEAD

▲ **To place a bead when working a right-side row,** ① simply work to the knit stitch you want to emboss, bring the yarn forward, and slide a bead up to the needle.

▲ ② Slip the knit stitch.

▲ ③ Bring the yarn to the back, leaving a bead on the front of the work.

▲ ④ Continue to knit.

▲ **To place a bead when working a wrong-side row,** work to the stitch you want to emboss, bring the yarn to the back, slide a bead up to the needle, slip the stitch purlwise, and bring the yarn back to the front, leaving a bead on the right side of the work. Continue to purl.

SLIPSTITCHING MULTIPLE BEADS

This is the technique used in the Beads-Go-Sporty Pullover (see page 88), and it may be worked on right- or wrong-side rows.

▲ Proceed as instructed in the Slipstitching a Single Bead section, but instead of bringing one bead up and slipping one stitch, ① bring up two beads and slip two stitches.

▲ ② Continue to knit.

INSPIRED SLIPSTITCH BEADING

Multiple Beads

Beads are placed on right-side rows to form a pattern on a stockinette stitch ground.

Single Beads

Ribbing is a great place to use beads. This is a 3/2 rib with beads placed both every other and every fourth row.

One bead is placed at the center of a textured pattern. Beads are placed on right-side rows.

Magic Mohair Beret

The beading is subtle on this beret, as you have to look at it under light to see the beadwork. Under that right light, though, it comes alive with sparkle.

Finished Measurements	21" (53 cm) circumference
Yarn	Wagtail Yarns 100% Kid Mohair (4 ply), 3.5 oz (100 g)/410 yd (375 m) *[Yarn band gauge: 24 stitches = 4" (10 cm) on US 3 (3.25 mm)]*; Slate Gray, 1 skein
Beads	Size 8° iridescent smoky crystal hex beads: about 450 (depending on how many rows are worked for the 3½" [9 cm] above the rib), 12 g
Needles	US 3 (3.25 mm) circular needle 16" (40 cm) long and set of 5 US 3 (3.25 mm) double-pointed needles, *or size you need to obtain correct gauge*
Gauge	24 stitches = 4" (10 cm) in stockinette stitch
Other Supplies	Big eye beading needle, stitch marker, tapestry needle, 10" (25 cm) dinner plate
Abbreviations	**SS1B** slipstitch 1 bead (see page 76)

•• BEADED SWIRL ••	STITCH PATTERN

ROUND 1: *(Yo, ssk) twice, P1, SS1B, P1, K5; repeat from *.

ROUND 2: Knit.

Repeat Rounds 1 and 2 for pattern.

Preparing the Yarn

• Using a big eye beading needle, string 450 beads onto yarn.

Knitting the Band

• **SETUP:** Cast on 126 stitches. Place marker and join into a round, being careful not to twist the stitches.
• **NEXT ROUNDS:** Work K1, P1 rib for 1" (2.5 cm).
• **INCREASE ROUND:** *K3, M1; repeat from *. *You now have* 168 stitches.

Beginning the Lace Pattern

• Work Rounds 1 and 2 of Beaded Swirl pattern for 3½" (9 cm), moving beginning-of-round marker 1 stitch to the left on every pattern round. (For example, to begin the next round, remove beginning-of-round marker, K1, and replace the marker. Then proceed with Round 1 of pattern.)

● ● **ALTERNATE DESIGN IDEA** ● ●

Highly contrasting beads underline the stitch pattern in this design. The swatch is knitted in Louet KidLin (linen/kid mohair/nylon), color 56-1702 White, with 8° gunmetal hex-cut beads.

Decreasing for the Crown

Note: Continue to move the beginning-of-round marker 1 stitch to the left on odd-numbered pattern rounds.

- **ROUND 1:** *Yo, ssk, yo, slip 1, K2tog, psso, P1, SS1B, P1, K4; repeat from *. *You now have* 154 stitches.
- **ROUND 2 AND ALL EVEN-NUMBERED ROUNDS:** Knit.
- **ROUND 3:** *Yo, ssk, yo, slip 1, K2tog, psso, P1, SS1B, P1, K3; repeat from *. *You now have* 140 stitches.
- **ROUND 5:** *Yo, ssk, yo, slip 1, K2tog, psso, P1, SS1B, P1, K2; repeat from *. *You now have* 126 stitches.
- **ROUND 7:** *Yo, ssk, yo, slip 1, K2tog, psso, P1, SS1B, P1, K1; repeat from *. *You now have* 112 stitches.
- **ROUND 9:** *Yo, ssk, yo, slip 1, K2tog, psso, P1, SS1B, P1; repeat from *. *You now have* 98 stitches.
- **ROUND 11:** Change to double-pointed needles. *Ssk, yo, ssk, P1, SS1B, P1; repeat from *. *You now have* 84 stitches.
- **ROUND 13:** *K1, ssk, P1, SS1B, P1; repeat from *. *You now have* 70 stitches.
- **ROUND 15:** *Ssk, P1, SS1B, P1; repeat from *. *You now have* 56 stitches.
- **ROUND 17:** *Ssk, P1, SS1B; repeat from *. *You now have* 42 stitches.
- **ROUND 19:** *Ssk, SS1B; repeat from *. *You now have* 28 stitches.
- **ROUND 21:** *Ssk; repeat from *. *You now have* 14 stitches.
- **ROUND 23:** Repeat Round 21. *You now have* 7 stitches.

Finishing

- Cut yarn, leaving an 8" (20 cm) tail.
- Thread tail onto tapestry needle and draw through remaining stitches twice. Pull up snug and fasten off on the inside.
- Completely wet the beret and gently squeeze out excess moisture.
- Shape beret over 10" (25 cm) dinner plate. Allow to dry completely before removing plate.

Beady-Eyed Cable Socks

This is one of my favorite uses of beads. Nestled inside cables, the beads peek out only from certain vantage points. Although the wool is superwash, I'd recommend hand washing these socks to maintain the luster of the beads.

Finished Measurements	8" (20 cm) circumference
Yarn	Lang Yarns Jawoll, 75% new wool/18% nylon/7% acrylic, 1.75 oz (50 g)/230 yd (210 m) *[Yarn band gauge: 30 stitches and 41 rows = 4" (10 cm) on US 2–3 (2.75–3.25 mm) needles]*; Color 084 Maroon, 2 skeins
Beads	Size 6° garnet seed beads: 240, 20 g
Needles	Sets of five US 2 (2.75 mm) and US 3 (3.25 mm) double-pointed needles, *or size you need to obtain the correct gauge*
Gauge	30 stitches = 4" (10 cm) in stockinette stitch on larger needle
Other Supplies	Big eye beading needle, two cable needles, tapestry needle
Abbreviations	**SS1B** slipstitch 1 bead (see page 76)

·· BEADED CABLE ··   STITCH PATTERN

ROUND 1: *K9, P3; repeat from *.

ROUND 2: *Slip 3 onto cable needle and hold in front, slip 3 onto second cable needle and hold in back, K3, K3 from second cable needle, K3 from first cable needle, P3; repeat from *.

ROUND 3: Repeat Round 1.

ROUNDS 4, 6, 8, AND 10: *K3, P1, SS1B, P1, K3, P3; repeat from *.

ROUNDS 5, 7, 9, AND 11: *K3, P1, K1, P1, K3, P3; repeat from *.

ROUND 12: *K9, P3; repeat from *.

Repeat Rounds 1–12 for pattern.

●● ALTERNATE DESIGN IDEA ●●

Beads look great with variegated sock yarn! This swatch is knitted in Classic Elite Alpaca Sox (alpaca/merino wool/nylon), color 1871 Candy Hearts, with 6° seed beads alternating pink and blue.

Preparing the Yarn

- Using a big eye beading needle, string 120 beads onto each skein of yarn.

Knitting the Leg

- **SETUP:** With two of the smaller needles held together to keep cast-on loose, cast on 60 stitches. Divide stitches onto four double-pointed needles as follows.

  Needles 1 and 3: 16 stitches each.

  Needles 2 and 4: 14 stitches each.

  Join into a round, being careful not to twist the stitches.

- **NEXT ROUNDS:** Using smaller needles, work K1, P1 rib for 1½" (2.5 cm).

- Change to larger needles, and increase and set up for cable as follows.

- **SETUP:** *K2, M1, K5, M1, P3; repeat from *. *You now have* 72 stitches:

  On needles 1 and 3: 21 stitches each.

  On needles 2 and 4: 15 stitches each.

Beginning Beaded Cable Pattern

- **ROUNDS 1–62:** Work Beaded Cable pattern for 5 full repeats. Work Rounds 1 and 2 once more.

Reducing Cable Stitches

- **NEXT ROUND:** *Slip 3 onto first cable needle and hold in front, slip 3 onto second cable needle and hold in back, K2tog, K1, K2tog, K1 from second cable needle, K3 from first cable needle, P3; repeat from *. *You now have* 60 stitches:

  On needles 1 and 3: 17 stitches each.

  On needles 2 and 4: 13 stitches each.

- **NEXT ROUND:** Work 1 round of knit the knits and purl the purls (see page 151).

(continued on next page)

Knitting the Heel Flap

- **SETUP:** Change to smaller needles and adjust stitches as follows:
  Move 3 stitches from needle 1 to needle 2, move 2 stitches from
  needle 3 to needle 4. Knit 14 stitches from needle 1 to needle 4.
  You now have
  On needle 1: 29 heel stitches.
  On needles 2 and 3: 31 instep stitches.
- **NEXT ROWS:** Work the heel flap back and forth on the 29 heel
  stitches as follows.
- **ROW 1 (WS):** Slip 1, P28.
- **ROW 2:** *Slip 1, K1; repeat from * to last stitch, K1.
- Repeat Rows 1 and 2 fourteen more times. *You now have* 15 chain
  stitches along each edge of the heel flap.

Turning the Heel

- **ROW 1 (WS):** Slip 1, P17, P2tog, turn.
- **ROW 2:** Slip 1, K7, ssk, turn.
- **ROW 3:** Slip 1, P7, P2tog, turn.
- Repeat Rows 2 and 3 until all stitches have been worked and you
  have 9 heel stitches remaining.

Knitting the Gussets

- **SETUP:**
  Needle 1: Using the needle with the heel stitches, pick up 15 stitches
  along side of heel flap.
  Needles 2 and 3 (instep):
  K4, (P3, K3, P1, K3) twice,
  P3, K4.
  Needle 4: With new needle,
  pick up 15 stitches along
  other side of heel flap and
  K4 heel stitches to same
  needle. *You now have* 70
  stitches:

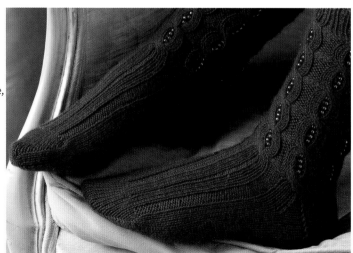

Needle 1: 20 stitches.

Needle 2: 16 stitches.

Needle 3: 15 stitches.

Needle 4: 19 stitches.

- ROUND 1:

  Needle 1: Knit to last 2 stitches, K2tog.

  Needles 2 and 3: Work instep stitches as established.

  Needle 4: Ssk, knit to end of round.

- ROUND 2: Knit.

- NEXT ROUNDS: Continue in this manner, decreasing at the end of needle 1 and the beginning of needle 4 and working 1 round even between decrease rounds until you have 60 stitches remaining.

Knitting the Foot

- Work even in stockinette stitch for sole, and in pattern as established for instep until foot measures 7" (18 cm), or 2" (5 cm) less than desired finished length.

Decreasing for the Toe

- SETUP: Move 1 stitch from needle 3 to needle 4 and 1 stitch from needle 2 to needle 3 and knit 1 round. *You now have* 15 stitches on each needle.

- ROUND 1:

  Needle 1: Knit to 3 stitches before end of needle 1, K2tog, K1.

  Needle 2: K1, ssk, knit to end of needle.

  Needle 3: Knit to last 3 stitches, K2tog, K1.

  Needle 4: K1, ssk, knit to end of needle.

- ROUND 2: Knit.

- Repeat Rounds 1 and 2 until 16 stitches remain.

Finishing

- Knit 4 stitches from needle 1 to needle 4. Slip 4 stitches from needle 3 to needle 2. *You now have* 16 stitches (2 needles with 8 stitches each).

- Graft the stitches together with Kitchener stitch (see page 151). Weave in ends using a tapestry needle.

Beads-Go-Sporty Pullover

Just because it's beaded doesn't mean it has to be flashy. The matte finish beads used for this sporty pullover are almost the same color as the yarn, and at first glance it looks like the beads could be a knitted texture.

Finished Measurements	36" (40", 44", 48") (91.5 cm [101.5 cm, 112 cm, 122 cm]) chest circumference
Yarn	Louet Gems, 100% merino wool, 3.5 oz (100 g)/225 yd (206 m) *[Yarn band gauge: 5–6 stitches = 1" (2.5 cm) on US 3–5 (3.25–3.75 mm) needles]*; Color 80-2523 Grape, 7 (7, 8, 8) skeins
Beads	Size 6° matte transparent smoky amethyst seed beads, 80–100 g (depending on size you're knitting)
Needles	US 5 (3.75 mm) straight and 16" (40 cm) circular needles, *or size you need to obtain correct gauge,* US 3 (3.25 mm) straight needles
Gauge	24 stitches and 36 rows = 4" (10 cm) in stockinette stitch on larger needle
Other Supplies	Big eye beading needle, scrap yarn for holders, stitch marker, tapestry needle
Abbreviations	**SS2B** slipstitch 2 beads (see page 76)

•• SEED STITCH ••	STITCH PATTERN

ROW 1 (RS): *K1, P1; repeat from *.

ROW 2: *P1, K1; repeat from *.

Repeat Rows 1 and 2 for pattern.

•• BEADED SQUARES ••	STITCH PATTERN

ROWS 1, 3, 5, 7, 9, AND 11 (RS): Seed 3, *K10, seed 3; repeat from *.

ROWS 2, 4, 10, AND 12: Seed 3, *P10, seed 3; repeat from *.

ROWS 6 AND 8: Seed 3, *P4, SS2B, P4, seed 3; repeat from *.

ROWS 13–16: Work in seed stitch.

Repeat Rows 1–16 for pattern.

Note: The first and third sizes will be centered on the 3 seed stitches between two blocks; the second and fourth sizes will be centered on a block.

Ⓢ 36"	Ⓜ 40"	Ⓛ 44"	Ⓧ 48"

Preparing the Yarn

• Wind yarn into balls. String 30" (76 cm) of beads onto each ball.

Knitting the Back

• SETUP: With larger straight needles, cast on

Ⓢ 107 sts	Ⓜ 120 sts	Ⓛ 133 sts	Ⓧ 146 sts

• ROWS 1–8: Work Seed Stitch for 8 rows.

• NEXT ROWS: Begin Beaded Squares pattern and work even until measurement above border is

Ⓢ 14" (35.5 cm)	Ⓜ 14" (35.5 cm)	Ⓛ 15¾" (40 cm)	Ⓧ 15¾" (40 cm)

• End with Row 14 of pattern.

● ● **ALTERNATE DESIGN IDEA** ● ●

The sporty sweater gets dressed up with a bright color and a sparkling transparent bead. The swatch is knitted in Gems, color 26 Crabapple, with transparent, pale pink beads.

| Ⓢ 36" | Ⓜ 40" | Ⓛ 44" | Ⓧ 48" |

Shaping the Armholes

- **SETUP:** Bind off 12 stitches at the beginning of the next two rows. *You now have*

| Ⓢ 83 sts | Ⓜ 96 sts | Ⓛ 109 sts | Ⓧ 122 sts |

- **NEXT ROWS:** Work even in pattern until piece measures 10" (25.5 cm) from armhole bind-off, ending with Row 14 of pattern.
- **NEXT ROW:**

Place on holder for Right Shoulder the first

| Ⓢ 24 sts | Ⓜ 28 sts | Ⓛ 32 sts | Ⓧ 36 sts |

Place on holder for Back Neck the next

| Ⓢ 35 sts | Ⓜ 40 sts | Ⓛ 45 sts | Ⓧ 50 sts |

Place on holder for Left Shoulder the last

| Ⓢ 24 sts | Ⓜ 28 sts | Ⓛ 32 sts | Ⓧ 36 sts |

Knitting the Front

- **NEXT ROWS:** Work as for back until measurement above border is

| Ⓢ 22" (56 cm) | Ⓜ 22" (56 cm) | Ⓛ 23¾" (60.5 cm) | Ⓧ 23¾" (60.5 cm) |

- End with Row 12 of pattern.

Shaping the Neck

- **NEXT ROW (ROW 13 OF PATTERN):**

Work in pattern and place on holder for Left Neck and Shoulder

| Ⓢ 32 sts | Ⓜ 36 sts | Ⓛ 40sts | Ⓧ 44 sts |

Bind off center

| Ⓢ 19 sts | Ⓜ 24 sts | Ⓛ 29 sts | Ⓧ 34 sts |

For Right Neck and Shoulder, work in pattern the next

| Ⓢ 32 sts | Ⓜ 36 sts | Ⓛ 40 sts | Ⓧ 44 sts |

- **NEXT ROW (WS):** Turn and work Row 14 on these stitches as established.
- **NEXT ROW:** Continuing on Right Neck and Shoulder stitches only, K1, ssk, work in pattern to end of row.
- **NEXT ROWS:** Repeat this decrease row on right-side rows seven more times. End with Row 14 of pattern.
- Place on holder for Right Shoulder the remaining

| Ⓢ 24 sts | Ⓜ 28 sts | Ⓛ 32 sts | Ⓧ 36 sts |

(continued on next page)

S 36"   **M** 40"   **L** 44"   **X** 48"

- **NEXT ROW:** With wrong side facing, return to needle from holder for the Left Front

  S 32 sts   **M** 36 sts   **L** 40 sts   **X** 44 sts

- Join yarn and work Row 14 of pattern as established.
- **NEXT ROW (RS):** Work in pattern to last 3 stitches, K2tog, K1.
- **NEXT ROWS:** Repeat this decrease row on right-side rows seven more times. End with Row 14 of pattern. Place on holder for Left Shoulder the remaining

  S 24 sts   **M** 28 sts   **L** 32 sts   **X** 36 sts

Knitting the Sleeves

- **SETUP:** With smaller needles, cast on 60 stitches.
- **NEXT ROWS:** Work in Seed Stitch until piece measures 1¾" (4.5 cm), or desired length for cuff.
- **NEXT ROW:** Change to larger needles and begin working Beaded Squares pattern, beginning and ending with K9 to center the pattern on the sleeve. Next Rows: Work 6 rows in pattern.
- **NEXT ROWS:** Increase 1 stitch at the beginning and end of the next row, then on every 4th row nine times. *You now have* 80 stitches.
- **NEXT ROWS:** Increase 1 stitch at the beginning and end of every 6th row twenty times. *You now have* 120 stitches.
- Work even to end with Row 16 of pattern. Place marker for underarm and work even for 2" (5 cm) more, ending with Row 4 of pattern. Sleeve measures about 21" (53 cm).
- Bind off.

S 36" **M** 40" **L** 44" **X** 48"

Assembling the Sweater

- Join Front and Back at shoulders, using the three-needle bind-off (see page 153). Block all pieces to schematic measurements.
- Using the tapestry needle, join sleeves to Front and Back along top edge of sleeve and along armhole shaping. Steam seams flat.
- Sew side and sleeve seams. Steam seams flat.

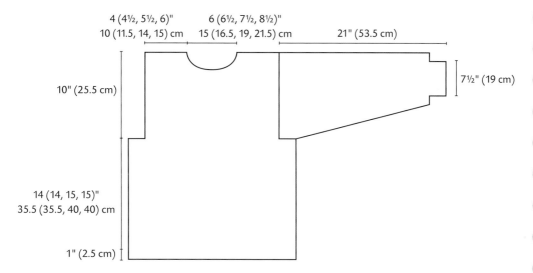

Finishing the Neck

- **SETUP:**

  With right side facing and using circular needle, join yarn at Left Shoulder and pick up and knit (see page 152) along Front neckline to Right Shoulder

  S 53 sts **M** 58 sts **L** 63 sts **X** 68 sts

  Return to needle from holder and work in Seed Stitch the Back

  S 35 sts **M** 40 sts **L** 45 sts **X** 50 sts

  Work in Seed Stitch the Front

  S 51 sts **M** 56 sts **L** 61 sts **X** 66 sts

  Work the last 2 Front stitches together in pattern. Place marker for end of round.

- **NEXT 5 ROUNDS:** Work even in Seed Stitch over

  S 87 sts **M** 97 sts **L** 107 sts **X** 117 sts

Note: When working Seed Stitch in the round, be certain to purl the knit stitches and knit the purl stitches on each subsequent round.

- Bind off loosely in pattern. Weave in ends. Steam neckline.

⑤ Carry-Along Bead Knitting

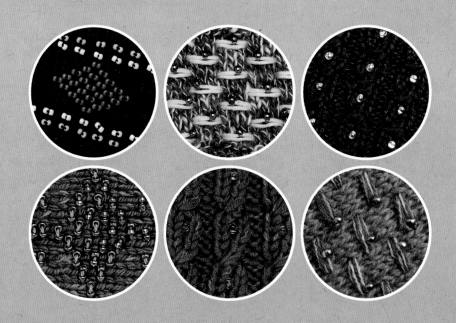

You can really expand your beading

horizons with this technique. Unlike the other methods presented in this book, with carry-along bead knitting you may use beads with holes that are too small to string on your main knitting yarn, as in the Drop-Bead Evening Shell (see page 102). You may work with small beads and use multiple beads over one stitch as in the Zulu Inspired Vest (see page 112). Or you may use both beads and the carry-along yarn to embellish a plain ground of stockinette stitch as in the Grape and Berries Pillow (see page 98). You may also choose beads that are much larger than a knit stitch and carry them along over multiple stitches.

For this technique, you'll need to string the beads onto a separate yarn that you "carry along" with the main yarn. This yarn may be the same color as the main yarn so it won't be seen, or it may be of a different color and texture to further embellish the work. You'll leave a bead in front of one or more stitches.

PLACING A BEAD OVER A SINGLE STITCH

Knit with both yarns held together to where you want to place a bead. ① Separate the two strands and bring the beaded yarn to the front of the work.

② With main yarn only, knit the stitch.

③ Bring the beaded yarn to the back and use both strands to continue knitting.

PLACING SEVERAL BEADS OVER A SINGLE STITCH

If the bead size allows, you may place two or more beads over a single stitch. This is how the Zulu Inspired Vest (page 112) was worked.

PLACING SEVERAL BEADS OVER MULTIPLE STITCHES

This method allows you to knit with beads that are much larger than one stitch.

Proceed as described for single-stitch beading, but knit two or more stitches with the carry-along yarn in front. Slide beads up to the width of the knitted stitches, bring the beaded yarn to the back, and use both strands to continue knitting.

CORRECTING MISTAKES

To add a missing bead, simply sew it in place with a strand of the carry-along yarn.

AVOIDING THE TWIST

When using a carry-along yarn, the most important thing is to keep the strands from twisting around each other. When you get to the place where you want a bead, it is impossible to insert a bead if the yarns are entwined by more than one or two twists. When knitting in the round, the strands will usually stay in place, but knitting back and forth may cause the problem.

I take up half the sofa when using this method, working with the ball of carry-along yarn on the sofa to my right and the main yarn on the sofa to my left.

At the end of a row, turn the work in a counterclockwise direction, so the two strands stay separated. Always make sure the yarns aren't twisted before you begin knitting a new row.

INSPIRED CARRY-ALONG BEADS

Seed beads are carried on a strand of fine silk yarn that is the same color as the main yarn. Several beads form loops when carried over two stitches.

Because you can use beads of any size, you can create interesting borders such as this one, with crystal-cut beads strung alternately with seed beads on a fine silk that matches the main yarn. Just be careful that your beads aren't too heavy for the garment.

Beads are strung on a multicolored metallic carry-along yarn. The contrasting yarn adds both texture and color, and the glass beads are placed randomly to add sparkle.

Grape and Berries Pillow

Here's a fun way to use beads on a carry-along yarn. Worked in a slipstitch pattern, the carry-along yarn gets "woven" in between stitches and is as much a part of the design as the beads. The pillow looks great and may possibly massage away a headache.

Finished Measurements	16" (40.5 cm) square
Yarn	MC: Peace Fleece DK, 30% mohair/70% wool, 4 oz (113 g)/350 yd (320 m) *[Yarn band gauge: 20 stitches = 4" (10 cm) on US 6 (4 mm)]*; Mir Atlantis Periwinkle, 1 skein
	CC: Ellie's Reclaimed Cashmere, 100% cashmere, 2.4 oz (68 g)/216 yd (198 m) [Yarn band gauge: 18 stitches = 4" (10 cm) on US 6–8 (4 mm–5 mm) needles]; Spring Mix, 1 skein
Beads	4mm fuchsia-lined smoky amethyst magatamas: 750, 65 g
Needles	US 7 (4.5 mm) straight needles, *or size you need to obtain correct gauge*
Gauge	24 stitches = 4" (10 cm) in beaded slipstitch, 21 stitches = 4" (10 cm) in stockinette stitch
Other Supplies	Big eye beading needle, 16" (40.5 cm) pillow form

·· WOVEN BERRIES ··   STITCH PATTERN

ROW 1 (RS): With MC, knit.

ROW 2: With MC, purl.

ROW 3: With CC, K1, *slip 3 wyib, slip 3 wyif; repeat from * to last 4 stitches, slip 3 wyib, K1.

ROW 4: With CC, K1, * slip 3 wyif, bead slip 3 wyib; repeat from * to last 4 stitches, slip 3 wyif, P1.

Repeat Rows 1–4 for pattern.

Note: The contrasting color (CC) is knitted only at the beginning of the row. All other stitches in the row are slipped with CC alternating between the front and back of the work to create the woven effect. On even-numbered (wrong-side) rows of CC, slide a bead up when the yarn is on the right side (bead slip 3 wyib).

● ● ALTERNATE DESIGN IDEA ● ●

Reverse the design by using a tweed or multicolored yarn for the background and a solid to carry the beads. The swatch is knitted in Farmhouse Yarn Silk Blend (silk/cotton/lamb's wool), Lavender, with Reynold's Soft Linen (flax/acrylic), color 0401 White, with the same beads that were used for the project.

Preparing the Yarn

- Using a big eye beading needle, string all the beads onto CC yarn.

Knitting the Front

- **SETUP:** With MC, cast on 95 stitches.
- **NEXT ROWS:** Work Rows 1–4 of stitch pattern until piece measures 15½" (39.5 cm), ending with a wrong-side row. Bind off.

Knitting the Back

- **SETUP:** With MC, cast on 80 stitches.
- **NEXT ROWS:** Work stockinette stitch until piece measures 15½" (39.5 cm), ending with a wrong-side row. Bind off.

Finishing

- Using a tapestry needle, sew front to back using a mattress stitch (see page 152) and leaving an opening to insert the pillow form.
- Insert pillow form through the opening and sew opening closed.

Drop-Bead Evening Shell

Here's a classic sleeveless shell that can go almost anywhere — kind of like the little black dress with pearls. But you can leave the pearls at home because clear crystal drop beads are knitted right into the mock turtleneck.

Finished Measurements	32½" (36½", 40½", 44", 48") (82.5 cm [92.5 cm, 103 cm, 112 cm, 122 cm]) chest circumference *Note:* This pattern is written for 100% bamboo yarn, which is very elastic when knitted. The shell is meant to be form-fitting, so choose a size very close (even slightly less) than the wearer's chest measurement.
Yarn	South West Trading Company Bamboo, 100% bamboo fiber, 3.5 oz (100 g)/250 yd (229 m) *[Yarn band gauge: 20 stitches and 32 rows = 4" (10 cm) on US 6 (4 mm) needles]*; Color 126 Black, 3 (4, 4, 5, 5) skeins
Beads	3.4mm clear crystal drop beads, 80
Needles	US 6 (4 mm) circular needle 24" (60 cm) long, *or size you need to obtain correct gauge;* circular needles one size smaller than gauge needle, 24" (60 cm) and 16" (40 cm) long; US 10.5 (6.5 mm) needle of any type for bind-off
Gauge	25 stitches and 36 rows = 4" (10 cm) on larger needles
Other Supplies	Big eye beading needle, 20 yd (18 m) size 10 black crochet cotton for carrying beads, two stitch markers, cotton string for holders, tapestry needle
Abbreviations	**YFB1** bring yarn forward with bead (see page 96) **C3R** knit the 3rd stitch, purl the 2nd stitch, knit the 1st stitch, and then drop all 3 stitches from needle

•• CROSSED RIB ••   STITCH PATTERN

ROUNDS 1–4: *K1, P1, K1, P2; repeat from *.

ROUND 5: *C3R, P2; repeat from *.

ROUND 6: Repeat Round 1.

Repeat Rounds 1–6 for pattern.

•• KNOT STITCH *(worked circularly)* ••   STITCH PATTERN

ROUNDS 1–6: Knit.

ROUND 7: K1, *(P3tog, K3tog, P3tog in next 3 stitches), K9; repeat from * to last 11 stitches, (P3tog, K3tog, P3tog in next 3 stitches), K8.

ROUNDS 8–14: Knit.

ROUND 15: K7, *(P3tog, K3tog, P3tog in next 3 stitches), K9; repeat from * to last 5 stitches, (P3tog, K3tog, P3tog in next 3 stitches), K2.

ROUND 16: Knit.

Repeat Rounds 1–16 for pattern.

•• KNOT STITCH *(worked flat)* ••   STITCH PATTERN

Continue knot pattern as established for circular knitting but purl all even-numbered (wrong-side) rows.

•• ALTERNATE DESIGN IDEA ••

This classic design would look great in almost any color. This swatch is knitted in Bamboo, color 148 Plum, with 3.4mm gold-lined crystal drop beads carried on a plum-colored lace-weight silk yarn.

S 32½" **M** 36½" **L** 40½" **X** 44" **XX** 48"

Stringing the Beads

• Using a big eye beading needle, string beads onto crochet cotton and set aside.

Knitting the Bottom Rib

• SETUP: With smaller 24" (60 cm) circular needle, cast on

S 200 sts **M** 225 sts **L** 250 sts **X** 270 sts **XX** 295 sts

Place a marker for left side and join into a round, being careful not to twist the stitches.

• NEXT ROUNDS: Work in Crossed Rib stitch until measurement from cast-on edge is

S 2½" (6.5 cm) **M** 2½" (6.5 cm) **L** 3" (7.5 cm) **X** 3½" (9 cm) **XX** 3½" (9 cm)

Knitting the Lower Body

• NEXT ROUND: Knit 1 round, evenly spacing and increasing

S 4 sts **M** 3 sts **L** 2 sts **X** 6 sts **XX** 5 sts

You now have

S 204 sts **M** 228 sts **L** 252 sts **X** 276 sts **XX** 300 sts

• NEXT ROUND: Place a marker for right side after knitting

S 102 sts **M** 114 sts **L** 126 sts **X** 138 sts **XX** 150 sts

• NEXT ROUNDS: Knit 4 rounds.

• NEXT ROUND: Change to larger needles and begin Knot Stitch pattern (worked circularly) with Round 7.

• NEXT ROUNDS: Continue in pattern as established until measurement from cast-on is

S 12" (30.5 cm) **M** 12" (30.5 cm) **L** 13" (33 cm) **X** 14" (35.5 cm) **XX** 14" (35.5 cm)

• End with either Round 8 or 16 of pattern.

Dividing Front and Back

• NEXT ROUND (RS ROW 1 OR 9):

Knit past the first (right-side) marker

S 6 sts **M** 7 sts **L** 8 sts **X** 9 sts **XX** 10 sts

Of the stitches just worked, place on holder for Right Underarm the last

S 12 sts **M** 14 sts **L** 16 sts **X** 18 sts **XX** 20 sts

Knit to end of round and place on holder for the Left Underarm the round's last

S 6 sts **M** 7 sts **L** 8 sts **X** 9 sts **XX** 10 sts

(continued on next page)

S 32½"	**M** 36½"	**L** 40½"	**X** 44"	**XX** 48"

and the round's first

S 6 sts	**M** 7 sts	**L** 8 sts	**X** 9 sts	**XX** 10 sts

Break yarn.

Place on a holder the Front

S 90 sts	**M** 100 sts	**L** 110 sts	**X** 120 sts	**XX** 130 sts

You now have on the needle for the Back

S 90 sts	**M** 100 sts	**L** 110 sts	**X** 120 sts	**XX** 130 sts

Knitting the Back

- **SETUP:** With wrong side of Back facing, join yarn at Left Underarm.
- **NEXT ROW (WS ROW 2 OR 10):** Continue with Knot Stitch pattern worked flat on Back

S 90 sts	**M** 100 sts	**L** 110 sts	**X** 120 sts	**XX** 130 sts

- Begin armhole shaping on next right-side row.

Shaping the Armholes

- **DECREASE ROW:** K1, ssk, work in pattern to last 3 stitches, K2tog, K1.
- **NEXT ROWS:** Continue in Knot Stitch pattern as established and work the decrease row every other row

S 5 times	**M** 5 times	**L** 6 times	**X** 7 times	**XX** 8 times

You now have

S 78 sts	**M** 88 sts	**L** 96 sts	**X** 104 sts	**XX** 112 sts

- **NEXT ROWS:** Continue in Knot Stitch pattern as established and work the decrease row every 4th row

S 4 times	**M** 4 times	**L** 5 times	**X** 5 times	**XX** 6 times

You now have

S 70 sts	**M** 80 sts	**L** 86 sts	**X** 94 sts	**XX** 100 sts

- **NEXT ROWS:** Continue in Knot Stitch pattern as established and repeat the decrease row every 6th row

S 2 times	**M** 3 times	**L** 3 times	**X** 3 times	**XX** 3 times

You now have

S 66 sts	**M** 74 sts	**L** 80 sts	**X** 88 sts	**XX** 94 sts

- **NEXT ROWS:** Continue even in pattern until measurement from underarm is

S 7¼" (18.5 cm)	**M** 7¾" (19.5 cm)	**L** 8" (20.5 cm)	**X** 8½" (21.5 cm)	**XX** 9" (23 cm)

S 32½" **M** 36½" **L** 40½" **X** 44" **XX** 48"

Shaping the Shoulders

- **NEXT 4 ROWS:** At the beginning of the next 4 rows, bind off

  S 5 sts **M** 5 sts **L** 6 sts **X** 7 sts **XX** 7 sts

- **NEXT 2 ROWS:** At the beginning of the next 2 rows, bind off

  S 5 sts **M** 7 sts **L** 6 sts **X** 7 sts **XX** 8 sts

- Place on holder for Back Neck the remaining

  S 36 sts **M** 40 sts **L** 44 sts **X** 46 sts **XX** 50 sts

Knitting the Front

- Place on needles for Front the held

  S 90 sts **M** 100 sts **L** 110 sts **X** 120 sts **XX** 130 sts

- With wrong side of Front facing, join yarn at Right Underarm. Work as for Back until piece is 14 rows below beginning of shoulder shaping, ending on a wrong-side row.

Shaping the Left Front Neck

- **NEXT ROW (RS):**

  Work in pattern

  S 23 sts **M** 25 sts **L** 26 sts **X** 28 sts **XX** 29 sts

  Place on holder for Front Neck the next

  S 20 sts **M** 24 sts **L** 28 sts **X** 32 sts **XX** 36 sts

  Place on separate holder for Right Front the remaining

  S 23 sts **M** 25 sts **L** 26 sts **X** 28 sts **XX** 29 sts

- **NEXT ROW (WS):** Work 1 row even.
- **NEXT ROWS:** Work in pattern to last 3 stitches, K2tog, K1. Repeat this decrease row every other row

  S 5 times **M** 5 times **L** 5 times **X** 4 times **XX** 4 times

- End with a wrong-side row. *You now have*

  S 17 sts **M** 19 sts **L** 20 sts **X** 23 sts **XX** 24 sts

(continued on next page)

Ⓢ 32½"   Ⓜ 36½"   Ⓛ 40½"   ⓧ 44"   ⓍⓍ 48"

Shaping the Left Shoulder

- **NEXT ROW (RS):**
  Bind off
  Ⓢ 5 sts   Ⓜ 5 sts   Ⓛ 6 sts   ⓧ 7 sts   ⓍⓍ 7 sts
  Work to last 3 stitches, K2tog, K1. *You now have*
  Ⓢ 11 sts   Ⓜ 13 sts   Ⓛ 13 sts   ⓧ 15 sts   ⓍⓍ 16 sts
- **NEXT ROW (WS):** Purl.
- **NEXT ROWS:** Repeat the last 2 rows once.
- Bind off remaining
  Ⓢ 5 sts   Ⓜ 7 sts   Ⓛ 6 sts   ⓧ 7 sts   ⓍⓍ 8 sts

Shaping the Right Front Neck

- **SETUP:** Return to needle from holder
  Ⓢ 23 sts   Ⓜ 25 sts   Ⓛ 26 sts   ⓧ 28 sts   ⓍⓍ 29 sts
- **NEXT 2 ROWS:** With right side facing, join yarn at Front Neck edge and work 2 rows even.
- **NEXT ROW:** K1, ssk, work to end of row.
- **NEXT ROWS:** Repeat this decrease row every other row
  Ⓢ 5 times   Ⓜ 5 times   Ⓛ 5 times   ⓧ 4 times   ⓍⓍ 4 times
- End with a right-side row. *You now have*
  Ⓢ 17 sts   Ⓜ 19 sts   Ⓛ 20 sts   ⓧ 23 sts   ⓍⓍ 24 sts

Shaping the Right Shoulder

- **NEXT ROW (WS):**
  Bind off
  Ⓢ 5 sts   Ⓜ 5 sts   Ⓛ 6 sts   ⓧ 7 sts   ⓍⓍ 7 sts
  Work to end of row.
- **NEXT ROW (RS):** K1, ssk, work to end of row.
- **NEXT ROWS:** Repeat the last 2 rows once.
- Bind off remaining
  Ⓢ 5 sts   Ⓜ 7 sts   Ⓛ 6 sts   ⓧ 7 sts   ⓍⓍ 8 sts

S 32½" **M** 36½" **L** 40½" **X** 44" **XX** 48"

Joining the Shoulders

• Using a tapestry needle, sew Front and Back Right and Left Shoulder pieces together.

Knitting the Collar

• **SETUP:** Return to needle from holder the Back Neck stitches.

Using the smaller 16" (40 cm) circular needle and holding beaded thread together with working yarn, join yarn at Right Back Neck and knit Back Neck

S 36 sts **M** 40 sts **L** 44 sts **X** 46 sts **XX** 50 sts

Pick up and knit (see page 152) 12 stitches along Left Front Neck.

Knit Front Neck

S 20 sts **M** 24 sts **L** 28 sts **X** 32 sts **XX** 36 sts

Pick up and knit 12 stitches along Right Front Neck. *You now have*

S 80 sts **M** 88 sts **L** 96 sts **X** 102 sts **XX** 110 sts

• Place a marker and join for circular knitting.

• **ROUND 1:** Work Round 1 of Crossed Rib pattern, increasing

S 0 sts **M** 2 sts **L** 4 sts **X** 3 sts **XX** 0 sts

• **ROUND 2:** *K1, YFB1, K1, P2; repeat from *.

• **NEXT ROUNDS:** Work Rounds 3–6 of Crossed Rib pattern. Continue as established until collar measures 3" (7.5 cm), ending with Round 3 of pattern.

• Bind off in pattern using the large bind-off needle.

Ⓢ 32½"   Ⓜ 36½"   Ⓛ 40½"   Ⓧ 44"   ⓍⓍ 48"

Knitting the Armhole Ribbing

• **SETUP:** Return to needle from holder the Right Underarm

Ⓢ 12 sts   Ⓜ 14 sts   Ⓛ 16 sts   Ⓧ 18 sts   ⓍⓍ 20 sts

• **NEXT ROUND:** Using the smaller 16" (40 cm) circular needle, join yarn at beginning of underarm stitches.

K2tog

Ⓢ 6 times   Ⓜ 7 times   Ⓛ 8 times   Ⓧ 9 times   ⓍⓍ 10 times

Around armhole, pick up and knit

Ⓢ 84 sts   Ⓜ 93 sts   Ⓛ 97 sts   Ⓧ 101 sts   ⓍⓍ 105 sts

Note: Pick-up rate is about 2 for every 3 stitches. *You now have*

Ⓢ 90 sts   Ⓜ 100 sts   Ⓛ 105 sts   Ⓧ 110 sts   ⓍⓍ 115 sts

• **NEXT ROUNDS:** Work Rounds 3–6 of Crossed Rib pattern and then work Rounds 1–3.

• Bind off loosely in pattern.

• Repeat for Left Armhole ribbing.

Finishing

• Using a tapestry needle, weave in ends.

KNOT STITCH

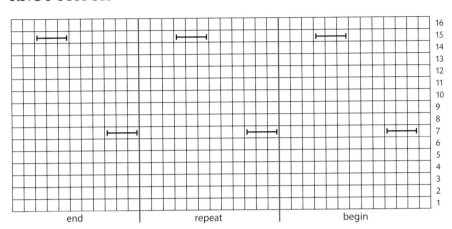

☐	Knit on RS, purl on WS
⊢━━⊣	P3tog, K3tog, P3tog

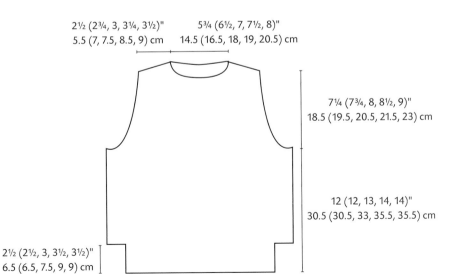

2½ (2¾, 3, 3¼, 3½)"
5.5 (7, 7.5, 8.5, 9) cm

5¾ (6½, 7, 7½, 8)"
14.5 (16.5, 18, 19, 20.5) cm

7¼ (7¾, 8, 8½, 9)"
18.5 (19.5, 20.5, 21.5, 23) cm

12 (12, 13, 14, 14)"
30.5 (30.5, 33, 35.5, 35.5) cm

2½ (2½, 3, 3½, 3½)"
6.5 (6.5, 7.5, 9, 9) cm

Zulu Inspired Vest

I got the idea for this vest from *Zulu Inspired Beadwork* by Diane Fitzgerald. Red, black, white, and green are used frequently in Zulu beadwork, and there is no shortage of diamond motifs. The beads are strung on black yarn and worked as two beads over one stitch. The black yarn peeks through between the beads, adding an extra dimension to the design.

Finished Measurements	36" (40", 44", 48", 52") (91.5 cm [101.5 cm, 112 cm, 122 cm, 132 cm]) chest circumference
Yarn	Rowan Classic Yarns Silk Wool DK, 50% merino wool/50% silk, 1.75 oz (50 g)/109 yd (100 m) *[Yarn band gauge: 22 stitches and 30 rows = 4" (10 cm) in stockinette stitch]*; MC: 312 Lip Gloss, 6 (7, 7, 8, 9) balls CC: 309 Black, 2 (3, 3, 3, 3) balls
Beads	Size 8° seed beads: 524 (568, 576, 616, 624), 14 g (15 g, 15 g, 16 g, 16 g) each of green and white; 1,000 (1,100, 1,100, 1,200, 1,200), 25 g (28 g, 28 g, 30 g, 30 g) red
Needles	US 7 (4.5 mm) circular needle 24" (60 cm) long, *or size you need to obtain correct gauge;* spare needle for three-needle bind-off; circular needle one size smaller than body needle 32" (80 cm) long for front border; circular needle two sizes smaller than body needle 16" (40 cm) long for armholes
Gauge	22 stitches and 30 rows = 4" (10 cm) in stockinette stitch
Other Supplies	Big eye beading needle, 150 yds (137 m) lace-weight black wool yarn for carrying beads, stitch markers, scrap yarn for holders, US D/3 (3.25 mm) crochet hook, tapestry needle
Abbreviations	**YFB2** yarn in front with 2 beads over 1 stitch (see page 96)

Note: The Fronts and Back are worked as one piece to the armholes, then separately to the shoulders. Stitches for the beaded border are picked up and knitted outward after the shoulder seams are joined.

● ● **ALTERNATE DESIGN IDEA** ● ●

The ethnic design is transformed with different colors of yarn and one color sparkly bead. The swatch is knitted in Silk Wool, colors 306 Greenwood and 307 Velvet, with purple-lined amethyst beads carried on a green lace-weight yarn.

S 36" **M** 40" **L** 44" **X** 48" **XX** 52"

Stringing the Beads

- Using a big eye beading needle, string beads onto the lace-weight wool in the following order of colors and quantities:

Green

S 262 **M** 284 **L** 288 **X** 308 **XX** 312

White

S 262 **M** 284 **L** 288 **X** 308 **XX** 312

Red

S 1,000 **M** 1,100 **L** 1,100 **X** 1,200 **XX** 1,200

White

S 262 **M** 284 **L** 288 **X** 308 **XX** 312

Green

S 262 **M** 284 **L** 288 **X** 308 **XX** 312

- Set aside.

Knitting the Lower Body

- SETUP: With larger needle and MC, cast on

  S 170 sts **M** 192 sts **L** 214 sts **X** 236 sts **XX** 258 sts

- NEXT 10 ROWS: Work garter stitch for 10 rows.
- NEXT ROWS: Change to stockinette stitch and work even until measurement from cast-on edge is

  S 11¾" (30 cm) **M** 12½" (32 cm) **L** 12½" (32 cm) **X** 13¾" (35 cm) **XX** 13¾" (35 cm)

- End with a wrong-side row.

Dividing for Underarms and Fronts

- NEXT ROW:

  Knit and then place on holder for Right Front

  S 22 sts **M** 27 sts **L** 32 sts **X** 37 sts **XX** 42 sts

  Knit and then place on holder for Right Underarm the next

  S 20 sts **M** 22 sts **L** 24 sts **X** 26 sts **XX** 28 sts

  Knit for Back the next

  S 86 sts **M** 94 sts **L** 102 sts **X** 110 sts **XX** 118 sts

  Place on holder for Left Underarm and Left Front the remaining

  S 42 sts **M** 49 sts **L** 56 sts **X** 63 sts **XX** 70 sts

S 36"   **M** 40"   **L** 44"   **X** 48"   **XX** 52"

Knitting the Back

• **NEXT ROW (WS):** Purl 1 row, working only on Back

   S 86 sts   **M** 94 sts   **L** 102 sts   **X** 110 sts   **XX** 118 sts

• **DECREASE ROW (RS):** Ssk, knit to last 2 stitches, K2tog.

• **NEXT ROWS:** Continuing in stockinette stitch, repeat this decrease row on right-side rows

   S 3 times   **M** 4 times   **L** 5 times   **X** 6 times   **XX** 7 times

   You now have

   S 78 sts   **M** 84 sts   **L** 90 sts   **X** 96 sts   **XX** 102 sts

• **NEXT ROWS:** Work even in pattern until measurement from underarm is

   S 9" (23 cm)   **M** 9½" (24 cm)   **L** 9½" (24 cm)   **X** 10" (25.5 cm)   **XX** 10" (25.5 cm)

• End with a wrong-side row.

Shaping the Back Neck

• **NEXT ROW:**

   Knit

   S 18 sts   **M** 20 sts   **L** 22 sts   **X** 24 sts   **XX** 26 sts

   Place on holder for Back Neck the next

   S 42 sts   **M** 44 sts   **L** 46 sts   **X** 48 sts   **XX** 50 sts

   Place on separate holder for Left Shoulder the next

   S 18 sts   **M** 20 sts   **L** 22 sts   **X** 24 sts   **XX** 26 sts

• **NEXT ROW (WS):** Purl 1 row, working only Right Shoulder

   S 18 sts   **M** 20 sts   **L** 22 sts   **X** 24 sts   **XX** 26 sts

• **DECREASE ROW (RS):** Knit to last 2 stitches, K2tog.

• **NEXT ROWS:** Continuing in stockinette stitch, repeat this decrease row on right-side rows

   S 2 more times   **M** 2 more times   **L** 3 more times   **X** 3 more times   **XX** 4 more times

• End with a wrong-side row. *You now have* for the Right Shoulder

   S 15 sts   **M** 17 sts   **L** 18 sts   **X** 20 sts   **XX** 21 sts

• Place these stitches on a holder.

• Return to needle from holder for Left Shoulder

   S 18 sts   **M** 20 sts   **L** 22 sts   **X** 24 sts   **XX** 26 sts

• **NEXT 2 ROWS:** With right side facing, join yarn and knit 1 row, then purl 1 row.

• **DECREASE ROW (RS):** Ssk, knit to end of row.

S 36" **M** 40" **L** 44" **X** 48" **XX** 52"

- **NEXT ROWS:** Continuing in stockinette stitch, repeat this decrease row on right-side rows
  - **S** 2 more times **M** 2 more times **L** 3 more times **X** 3 more times **XX** 4 more times
- End with a wrong-side row. *You now have* for the Left Shoulder
  - **S** 15 sts **M** 17 sts **L** 18 sts **X** 20 sts **XX** 21 sts
- Place these stitches on a holder.

Knitting the Right Front

- **SETUP:** Return to needle from holder for Right Front
  - **S** 22 sts **M** 27 sts **L** 32 sts **X** 37 sts **XX** 42 sts
- **NEXT ROW (WS):** With wrong side facing, join yarn and purl 1 row.
- **DECREASE ROW (RS):** Knit to last 2 stitches, K2tog.
- **NEXT ROWS:** Continuing in stockinette stitch, repeat this decrease row on right-side rows
  - **S** 2 more times **M** 3 more times **L** 4 more times **X** 5 more times **XX** 6 more times
- End with a wrong-side row. *You now have*
  - **S** 19 sts **M** 23 sts **L** 27 sts **X** 31 sts **XX** 35 sts
- **NEXT ROW:** Ssk (Front Neck decrease), knit to last 2 stitches, K2tog.
- Armhole shaping is complete. *You now have*
  - **S** 17 sts **M** 21 sts **L** 25 sts **X** 29 sts **XX** 33 sts
- **NEXT ROWS:** Continuing in stockinette stitch, repeat the Front Neck decrease only every 4th row
  - **S** 0 times **M** 0 times **L** 0 times **X** 4 times **XX** 12 times
  You now have
  - **S** 17 sts **M** 21 sts **L** 25 sts **X** 25 sts **XX** 21 sts
- **NEXT ROWS:** Continuing in stockinette stitch, repeat the Front Neck decrease only every 6th row
  - **S** 0 times **M** 0 times **L** 5 times **X** 5 times **XX** 0 times
  You now have
  - **S** 17 sts **M** 21 sts **L** 20 sts **X** 20 sts **XX** 21 sts
- **NEXT ROWS:** Continuing in stockinette stitch, repeat the Front Neck decrease only every 8th row
  - **S** 2 times **M** 4 times **L** 2 times **X** 0 times **XX** 0 times

(continued on next page)

| **S** 36" | **M** 40" | **L** 44" | **X** 48" | **XX** 52" |

You now have for the Right Shoulder

| **S** 15 sts | **M** 17 sts | **L** 18 sts | **X** 20 sts | **XX** 21 sts |

• Continue even until you have the same number of rows to Right Shoulder as Back.
• Place these stitches on a holder.

Knitting the Left Front

• **SETUP**: Return to needle from holder for the Left Underarm and Left Front

| **S** 42 sts | **M** 49 sts | **L** 56 sts | **X** 63 sts | **XX** 70 sts |

• **NEXT ROW (RS)**:

With right side facing, join yarn and knit and place on holder for Left Underarm

| **S** 20 sts | **M** 22 sts | **L** 24 sts | **X** 26 sts | **XX** 28 sts |

Knit the Left Front

| **S** 22 sts | **M** 27 sts | **L** 32 sts | **X** 37 sts | **XX** 42 sts |

• **NEXT ROW (WS)**: Purl 1 row.
• **DECREASE ROW (RS)**: Ssk, knit to end of row.
• **NEXT ROWS**: Continuing in stockinette stitch, repeat this decrease row on right-side rows

| **S** 2 more times | **M** 3 more times | **L** 4 more times | **X** 5 more times | **XX** 6 more times |

• End with a wrong-side row. *You now have*

| **S** 19 sts | **M** 23 sts | **L** 27 sts | **X** 31 sts | **XX** 35 sts |

• **NEXT ROW**: Ssk, knit to last 2 stitches, K2tog (Front Neck decrease). Armhole shaping is now complete. *You now have*

| **S** 17 sts | **M** 21 sts | **L** 25 sts | **X** 29 sts | **XX** 33 sts |

• **NEXT ROWS**: Continuing in stockinette stitch, repeat the Front Neck decrease only every 4th row

| **S** 0 times | **M** 0 times | **L** 0 times | **X** 4 times | **XX** 12 times |

You now have

| **S** 17 sts | **M** 21 sts | **L** 25 sts | **X** 25 sts | **XX** 21 sts |

• **NEXT ROWS**: Continuing in stockinette stitch, repeat the Front Neck decrease only every 6th row

| **S** 0 times | **M** 0 times | **L** 5 times | **X** 5 times | **XX** 0 times |

You now have

| **S** 17 sts | **M** 21 sts | **L** 20 sts | **X** 20 sts | **XX** 21 sts |

S 36"   **M** 40"   **L** 44"   **X** 48"   **XX** 52"

- **NEXT ROWS:** Continuing in stockinette stitch, repeat the front neck decrease only every 8th row

  S 2 times   **M** 4 times   **L** 2 times   **X** 0 times   **XX** 0 times

  You now have for the Left Shoulder

  S 15 sts   **M** 17 sts   **L** 18 sts   **X** 20 sts   **XX** 21 sts

- **NEXT ROWS:** Continue even until you have the same number of rows to Left Shoulder as Back.
- Place these stitches on a holder.

Joining the Shoulders

- With right sides together, join Front and Back Shoulder pieces together with the three-needle bind-off (see page 153).

Knitting the Border

Note: When picking up stitches for the border, the pick-up rate is about 3 for every 4 stitches.

- **SETUP:**

  With needle one size smaller, CC yarn, and right side facing, begin at the lower right front edge and pick up and knit (see page 152) 5 stitches along edge of garter stitch border.

  Pick up and knit to the shoulder

  S 107 sts   **M** 117 sts   **L** 117 sts   **X** 126 sts   **XX** 126 sts

  Pick up and knit 1 stitch in shoulder seam.

  Pick up and knit between the seam and Back Neck holder

  S 3 sts   **M** 3 sts   **L** 4 sts   **X** 4 sts   **XX** 5 sts

  From the holder, knit Back Neck

  S 42 sts   **M** 44 sts   **L** 46 sts   **X** 48 sts   **XX** 50 sts

  To the seam, pick up and knit

  S 3 sts   **M** 3 sts   **L** 4 sts   **X** 4 sts   **XX** 5 sts

  Pick up and knit 1 stitch in shoulder seam.

  Pick up and knit to the border

  S 107 sts   **M** 117 sts   **L** 117 sts   **X** 126 sts   **XX** 126 sts

(continued on next page)

S 36"   **M** 40"   **L** 44"   **X** 48"   **XX** 52"

Pick up and knit 5 stitches along garter stitch border. *You now have*

S 274 sts   **M** 296 sts   **L** 300 sts   **X** 320 sts   **XX** 324 sts

• NEXT ROWS: Knit 3 rows, decreasing 1 stitch at center back on 2nd row. *You now have*

S 273 sts   **M** 295 sts   **L** 299 sts   **X** 319 sts   **XX** 323 sts

Knitting the Beaded Pattern

• From this point, work with the CC yarn held together with beaded yarn.
• ROW 1 (RS): K6, *YFB2, K1; repeat from * to last 5 stitches, K5.
• ROW 2: K5, purl to last 5 stitches, K5.
• ROW 3: Repeat Row 1.

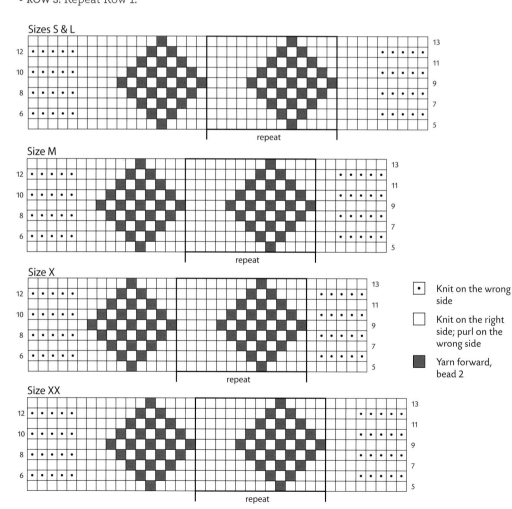

Sizes S & L

Size M

Size X

Size XX

repeat

• Knit on the wrong side

☐ Knit on the right side; purl on the wrong side

▪ Yarn forward, bead 2

ⓢ 36"	Ⓜ 40"	Ⓛ 44"	Ⓧ 48"	ⓍⓍ 52"

- **ROW 4:** Repeat Row 2, increasing 1 stitch at center back.
- **ROW 5:** Knit

ⓢ 13 sts	Ⓜ 11 sts	Ⓛ 13 sts	Ⓧ 10 sts	ⓍⓍ 12 sts

YFB2, *K12, YFB2; repeat from * to last

ⓢ 13 sts	Ⓜ 11 sts	Ⓛ 13 sts	Ⓧ 10 sts	ⓍⓍ 12 sts

Knit to end of row.
- **ROW 6:** K5, purl

ⓢ 7 sts	Ⓜ 5 sts	Ⓛ 7 sts	Ⓧ 4 sts	ⓍⓍ 6 sts

YFB2, P1, YFB2, *P10, YFB2, P1, YFB2; repeat from * to last

ⓢ 12 sts	Ⓜ 10 sts	Ⓛ 12 sts	Ⓧ 9 sts	ⓍⓍ 11 sts

Purl

ⓢ 7 sts	Ⓜ 5 sts	Ⓛ 7 sts	Ⓧ 4 sts	ⓍⓍ 6 sts

Knit 5.
- **ROW 7:** Knit

ⓢ 11 sts	Ⓜ 9 sts	Ⓛ 11 sts	Ⓧ 8 sts	ⓍⓍ 10 sts

(YFB2, K1) twice, YFB2, *K8, (YFB2, K1) twice, YFB2; repeat from * to last

ⓢ 11 sts	Ⓜ 9 sts	Ⓛ 11 sts	Ⓧ 8 sts	ⓍⓍ 10 sts

Knit to end of row.
- **ROW 8:** K5, purl

ⓢ 5 sts	Ⓜ 3 sts	Ⓛ 5 sts	Ⓧ 2 sts	ⓍⓍ 4 sts

(YFB2, K1) three times, YFB2, *P6, (YFB2, K1) three times, YFB2; repeat from * to last

ⓢ 10 sts	Ⓜ 8 sts	Ⓛ 10 sts	Ⓧ 7 sts	ⓍⓍ 9 sts

Purl

ⓢ 5 sts	Ⓜ 3 sts	Ⓛ 5 sts	Ⓧ 2 sts	ⓍⓍ 4 sts

Knit 5.
- **ROW 9:** Knit

ⓢ 9 sts	Ⓜ 7 sts	Ⓛ 9 sts	Ⓧ 6 sts	ⓍⓍ 8 sts

(YFB2, K1) four times, YFB2, *K4, (YFB2, K1) four times, YFB2; repeat from * to last

ⓢ 9 sts	Ⓜ 7 sts	Ⓛ 9 sts	Ⓧ 6 sts	ⓍⓍ 8 sts

Knit to end of row.
- **ROW 10:** Repeat Row 8.
- **ROW 11:** Repeat Row 7.
- **ROW 12:** Repeat Row 6.
- **ROW 13:** Repeat Row 5.

(continued on next page)

Ⓢ 36"	Ⓜ 40"	Ⓛ 44"	✕ 48"	✕✕ 52"

- ROW 14: Repeat Row 2, decreasing 1 stitch at center back.
- ROW 15: Repeat Row 1.
- ROW 16: Repeat Row 2.
- ROW 17: Repeat Row 1.
- ROW 18: Repeat Row 2.
- ROWS 19–22: Knit 4 rows. Bind off loosely purlwise (see page 153).

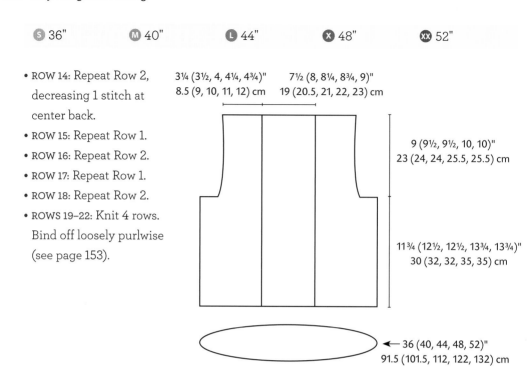

3¼ (3½, 4, 4¼, 4¾)"
8.5 (9, 10, 11, 12) cm

7½ (8, 8¼, 8¾, 9)"
19 (20.5, 21, 22, 23) cm

9 (9½, 9½, 10, 10)"
23 (24, 24, 25.5, 25.5) cm

11¾ (12½, 12½, 13¾, 13¾)"
30 (32, 32, 35, 35) cm

← 36 (40, 44, 48, 52)"
91.5 (101.5, 112, 122, 132) cm

Knitting the Armhole Binding

Note: For the armhole binding, the pick-up rate is about 3 for every 4 stitches.

- SETUP: Move the underarm stitches from the holder to the smallest circular needle. With MC, beginning at center of held underarm stitches (K2, K2tog) twice.
  Knit

Ⓢ 2 sts	Ⓜ 3 sts	Ⓛ 4 sts	✕ 5 sts	✕✕ 6 sts

Pick up and knit along armhole edge to shoulder

Ⓢ 48 sts	Ⓜ 51 sts	Ⓛ 51 sts	✕ 54 sts	✕✕ 54 sts

Pick up and knit from shoulder down to remaining underarm stitches on holder

Ⓢ 48 sts	Ⓜ 51 sts	Ⓛ 51 sts	✕ 54 sts	✕✕ 54 sts

Knit

Ⓢ 2 sts	Ⓜ 3 sts	Ⓛ 4 sts	✕ 5 sts	✕✕ 6 sts

(K2tog, K2) twice.

You now have

Ⓢ 112 sts	Ⓜ 120 sts	Ⓛ 122 sts	✕ 130 sts	✕✕ 132 sts

- NEXT 3 ROWS: Purl 1 round, knit 1 round, purl 1 round.
- Bind off.

Finishing

- Make three bobble buttons with smallest needle and CC yarn as follows:

  Cast on 1 stitch, leaving a 4" (10 cm) tail.

  Knit into the front, back, front, back, and front of the stitch. *You now have* 5 stitches.
- **NEXT ROWS:** Work 5 rows in stockinette stitch, beginning and ending with a purl row.
- **NEXT ROW:** With right side facing, slip the second, third, fourth, and fifth stitches one at a time over the first stitch. Break yarn, leaving a 4" (10 cm) tail, and pull the tail through the remaining stitch. Tie the tails together with a square knot.
- Make two more buttons.
- Attach one button on the edge of the left front border near the beginning of the neck shaping, one button about 4½ to 5" (11 to 13 cm) from bottom, and one button evenly spaced between the others.
- The vest is meant to be worn with an open space at the center front. Try on the vest to determine how much space you want between the borders.
- Use a crochet hook to anchor a length of CC yarn opposite the buttons, make a crochet chain (see page 150) twice the length of the desired opening, and anchor the end of the chain to the same place as the beginning, forming a button loop. Weave in ends using a tapestry needle.

⑥ Hook Bead Knitting

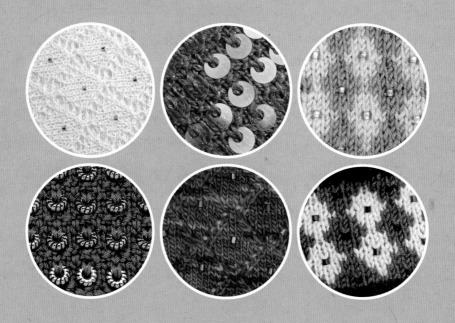

I first read about this technique in *Principles of Knitting* by June Hemmons Hiatt. Unlike all the other techniques in this book, this method doesn't require that you pre-string the beads. When you get to the stitch where you want a bead, you slip it right onto that stitch with a crochet hook.

When I first experimented with this method, I used large beads that would slip over the crochet hooks I had on hand. But when I bought a set of tiny steel crochet hooks, I found I could use seed beads, as in the Wedding Stole (see page 138). Because the bead is slipped over the entire stitch, beads lie straight up and down. This is important for knitting with paillettes, as in the Mermaid Shoulder Bag (see page 128), as well as with asymmetrical beads of any sort. I chose this method when working two-color stranded knitting, as in the Beady Tam (see page 134). (It's enough of a chore to keep the two balls of yarn under control, never mind beads, too!)

It may take a bit of experimenting to find the right combination of yarn, bead, and hook sizes, but once you do, there's no end to what you can accomplish.

HOOKING A BEAD

Knit to the stitch you want to bead. ① Pick up a bead with a crochet hook and pull the stitch off the needle with the crochet hook.

② Pull the stitch through the bead.

③ Place the stitch back on the needle.

Now, either knit the beaded stitch or slip it. I usually prefer to slip this stitch; knitting it usually makes a very tight stitch, which pushes the bead down into the fabric.

BEAD PLACEMENT BY ROWS

This swatch was knitted with the lace pattern used in the Wedding Stole (see page 138). Beads were placed in Rows 7 and 15, right in the center of the diamond motifs. Notice how the beads seem to gravitate toward the bottom of the diamonds.

In this sample, beads were placed on Rows 1 and 9, two rows above the exact center of the diamonds. The beads appear to sit closer to the center of the design. This is how the Wedding Stole is knitted.

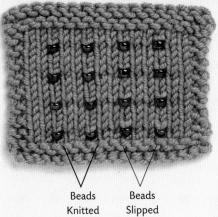

Beads
Knitted

Beads
Slipped

KNITTING VS. SLIPPING

In the swatch at the left, the two columns of beads on the right were worked with the beaded stitches slipped, and for the columns on the left, the beaded stitches were knitted. Notice how the beads on the right float on the surface, while the beads on the left are embedded in the fabric.

SLIPSTITCH BEADING VS. HOOK BEAD KNITTING

The bottom two rows of paillettes are hooked onto the stitches, making them line up in perfectly vertical rows. The paillettes in the top two rows were pre-strung and incorporated with slipstitch beading. Not only do they lie askew, they can easily flip from side to side or twist on the stitch.

Slipstitch
Beading

Hook Bead
Knitting

INSPIRED HOOK BEAD KNITTING

With hook bead knitting, you may embellish your knitting with charms with a loop at the top, shank-backed buttons, or beads shaped like donuts or disks.

Mermaid Shoulder Bag

Paillettes are just like scales on marine life, only shiny. Hooking all the paillettes is not a speedy task, but the end result is worth the effort. And it's the only way to make them lie flat on the surface of the knitted fabric. Lined with heavy-duty interfacing, this purse is both practical and chic.

Finished Measurements	11" (28 cm) wide × 8" (20.5 cm) tall × 3" (7.5 cm) deep
Yarn	Blue Heron Rayon Metallic, 88% rayon/12% metallic, 8 oz (227 g)/550 yd (503 m) [*Yarn band gauge: 18–20 stitches = 4" (10 cm) on US 7 (4.5 mm)*]; Deep Blue Sea, 1 skein
Beads	10mm iridescent blue large-hole paillettes, 1,000-count bag
Needles	US 3 (3.25 mm) circular needle 24" (60 cm) long, *or size you need to obtain correct gauge*
Gauge	30 stitches and 48 rounds = 4" (10 cm) in pattern
Other Supplies	US J/10 (6 mm) crochet hook , ½ yd (.5 m) double-sided stiff fusible interfacing, ½ yd (.5 m) lining fabric, cotton string for holders, sewing needle and coordinating sewing thread, tapestry needle, two 1½" (4 cm) D-rings
Abbreviations	**HB** hook bead (see page 126)

Note: The base of the bag is knit back and forth, then stitches are picked up around all sides, and the rest of the bag is knit in the round. To help mark the "seams," a purl stitch is worked between each section.

● ● ALTERNATE DESIGN IDEA ● ●

Don't like sequins? The same pattern produces a completely different design with silver spacers. The swatch is knitted in Filatura Di Crosa Luxury (silk), color 21 Blue-Gray, with 8mm silver spacer beads.

•• SEQUINED SEED STITCH *(worked circularly)* ••	STITCH PATTERN

ROUND 1: *K1, P1; repeat from * to last stitch, K1.

ROUND 2: *P1, K1, repeat from * to last stitch, P1.

ROUNDS 3 AND 4: Knit.

ROUND 5: *K2, HB; repeat from * to last 2 stitches, K2.

ROUND 6: Knit.

Repeat Rounds 1–6 for pattern.

•• SEED STITCH *(worked flat)* ••	STITCH PATTERN

ROW 1: *K1, P1; repeat from * to last stitch, K1.

Repeat Row 1 for pattern.

Knitting the Base of the Bag

- SETUP: Cast on 77 stitches. Work back and forth in seed stitch until piece measures 3" (7.5 cm) from beginning.

Knitting the Body of the Bag

- SETUP: Knit 77 stitches for front of bag, place marker (pm), pick up and knit (see page 152) 25 stitches along first short side of base, pm, pick up and knit 77 stitches for back of bag, pm, pick up and knit 25 stitches along second short side of base, pm. *You now have* 204 stitches.
- NEXT ROUNDS: Work Rounds 1–6 of Sequined Seed stitch as follows: *Work pattern over 77 stitches, slip marker (sm), P1, work pattern over 23 stitches, P1, sm; repeat from * once more.
- NEXT ROUNDS: Continue in pattern as established until you have completed 9 full repeats of pattern, ending with Round 6. The piece measures about 4½" (11.5 cm) from the base.

Decreasing the Sides

- NEXT ROUND: *Work pattern over 77 stitches, sm, P1, ssk, work in pattern to 3 stitches before next marker, K2tog, P1, sm; repeat from * once more.
- NEXT ROUNDS: Work Rounds 2–6 of Sequined Seed stitch pattern as established, adjusting placement of paillettes as necessary for the decreases.
- Repeat this sequence six more times.
  You now have 11 stitches remaining between the side markers, you've completed 16 pattern repeats, and the piece measures about 8" (20.5 cm) from the base.

Knitting the Top of the Bag

- **SETUP:** Purl 77 front bag stitches. Place next 11 stitches on a holder for the first strap, place next 77 stitches on separate holder for back of bag, and place remaining 11 stitches on another holder for the second strap.
- **NEXT ROUNDS:** Work in Seed Stitch back and forth over 77 front stitches to form a ¾" (2 cm) flap. Bind off.
- Place 77 back stitches on needle and work as for front.

Knitting the Straps

- Place 11 held stitches on needle and work back and forth in Seed Stitch until first strap measures 22" (56 cm), or desired length. Bind off.
- Repeat for second strap.
- Weave in ends using a tapestry needle.

Preparing the Lining

- Using the illustration on the opposite page as a guide, cut:
  One piece of interfacing 11" (28 cm) by 3" (7.5 cm)
  Two pieces of interfacing 11" (28 cm) by 8" (20.5 cm)
  Two pieces of interfacing 8" (20.5 cm) tall and 3" (7.5 cm) wide at the bottom, straight for 4½" (11.5 cm), and tapering to 2" (5 cm) wide at the top
  Twice as many lining pieces as described above, adding ½" (1.3 cm) seam allowance on all sides
- Following manufacturer's directions, apply lining fabric to both sides of all pieces, leaving a ½" (1.3 cm) seam allowance in lining on all sides of each piece.
- Assemble the lining by stitching the sides to the fronts and backs with sewing needle and thread. Then add the base.
- Place the lining into the knitted bag and adjust the fit.
- Fold top lining seam allowance toward knitted bag and stitch bag along top of lining, matching the purl ridge at the base of the flap to the edge of the lining.

Finishing

• Stitch front and back flaps together for about 1" (2.5 cm) on each end.

• Slide the D-rings onto the end of one strap, fold the strap back about 1" (2.5 cm) to the inside, encasing the D-rings, and stitch in place.

• Slide second strap through the D-rings and adjust as desired.

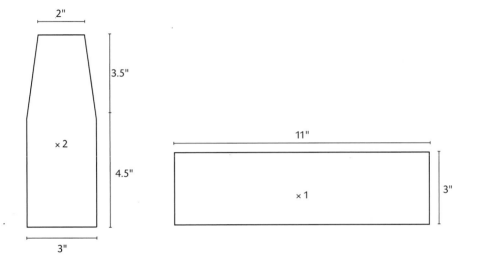

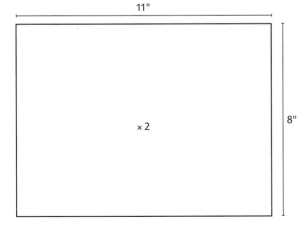

Beady Tam

This hat is a cross between a balmoral, with its two-colored band, and a tam o'shanter, with its small circular top. The beads add a prominent dot to the two-color pattern when placed on the white motifs, and they add shine when placed on the brown motifs.

Finished Measurements	To fit an adult woman's head, 22" (56 cm) circumference
Yarn	GGH Tajmahal, 70% merino wool/22% silk/8% cashmere, .88 oz (25 g)/ 93 yd (85 m) *[Yarn band gauge: 27 stitches and 36 rows = 4" (10 cm) on US 3–4 (3 mm–3.5 mm) needles]* MC: #13 Black, 3 balls CA: #1 Cream, 1 ball CB: #32 Brown, 1 ball
Beads	Size 8° black cut cylinder beads: 125, 4 g
Needles	US 3 (3.25 mm) circular needle 16" (40 cm) long and set of five US 3 (3.25 mm) double-pointed needles, *or size you need to obtain correct gauge*
Gauge	27 stitches = 4" (10 cm) in stockinette stitch
Other Supplies	US 14 (0.75 mm) crochet hook, tapestry needle
Abbreviations	**HB** hook bead (see page 126)

Knitting the Band

- **SETUP:** With MC and circular needle, cast on 150 stitches. Join into a round, being careful not to twist the stitches.
- **NEXT ROUNDS:** Work stockinette stitch (knit every round) until piece measures 2½" (6.5 cm) from cast-on edge.
- Purl 1 round. This round forms the turning ridge.
- Continue with MC for 8 more rounds.

Beginning the Color Pattern

- Following the chart, cut MC, join CA, and work two-color pattern, hooking beads in place as indicated and joining CB when needed.

Increasing the Crown

- **SETUP:** Cut CA and CB, join MC, and knit 1 round, increasing 2 stitches. *You now have* 152 stitches.
- Begin increasing for the top of the hat as follows.
- **INCREASE ROUND 1:** *K4, M1; repeat from *. *You now have* 190 stitches.
- **NEXT ROUNDS:** Knit 6 rounds even.
- **INCREASE ROUND 2:** *K5, M1; repeat from *. *You now have* 228 stitches.
- **NEXT ROUNDS:** Knit 13 rounds even.

●● **ALTERNATE DESIGN IDEA** ●●

Use pastel shades to transform this design into one that says "soft." The swatch is knitted in Tajmahal, colors 1 Cream, 8 Pink, and 15 Green with 6° transparent, pale pink seed beads.

Decreasing Top of Crown

- **DECREASE ROUND 1:** *K4, K2tog; repeat from *. *You now have* 190 stitches.
- **NEXT ROUNDS:** Knit 6 rounds even.
- **DECREASE ROUND 2:** *K3, K2tog; repeat from *. You now have 152 stitches.
- **NEXT ROUNDS:** Knit 6 rounds even.
- **DECREASE ROUND 3:** *K2, K2tog; repeat from *. *You now have* 114 stitches.
- **NEXT ROUNDS:** Knit 6 rounds even.
- **DECREASE ROUND 4:** *K1, K2tog; repeat from *. *You now have* 76 stitches.
- **NEXT ROUNDS:** Knit 6 rounds even.
- **DECREASE ROUND 5:** *K2tog; repeat from *. *You now have* 38 stitches.
- **NEXT ROUNDS:** Knit 2 rounds even.
- **DECREASE ROUND 6:** *K2tog; repeat from *. *You now have* 19 stitches.
- **NEXT ROUND:** Knit 1 round even.
- **FINAL DECREASE ROUND:** *K1, K2tog; repeat from *, K1. *You now have* 10 stitches.

Finishing

- Cut yarn, leaving an 8" (20 cm) tail.
- Thread the tail onto a tapestry needle and draw through remaining stitches twice. Pull up snug and fasten off on the inside. Weave in ends.
- Thread tapestry needle with MC. Fold hem to inside and sew in place.

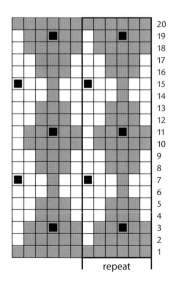

Knit with color A

Knit with color B

■ Hook bead

repeat

Wedding Stole

Knitted in white with gold beads, this shawl is the perfect gift for a winter bride. Knitted in your favorite color, it's a perfect gift for yourself. I chose to hook beads on this stole to save wear and tear on the very long skeins.

Finished Measurements	16" × 80" (41 cm × 203 cm) unblocked; 20" × 76" (51 cm × 193 cm) blocked
Yarn	Alpaca with a Twist Fino, 70% baby alpaca/30% silk, 3.5 oz (100 g)/ 875 yds (800 m) *[Yarn band gauge: 28 stitches = 4" (10 cm) on US 3 (3.25 mm) needle]*; Color 0099 Ivory, 2 skeins
Beads	Size 10° silver-lined gold seed beads, 25 g
Needles	US 2 (2.5 mm) straight needles, *or size you need to obtain correct gauge*
Gauge	27 stitches = 4" (10 cm) in pattern, blocked
Other Supplies	US 14 (0.75 mm) crochet hook, tapestry needle, rustproof pins
Abbreviations	**HB** hook bead (see page 126) **p2sso** pass 2 slipped stitches over last stitch on needle **sl2tog** slip 2 stitches together knitwise

•• DIAMOND LACE PATTERN ••	STITCH PATTERN

ROW 1: K1, *yo, ssk, K2, HB, K2, K2tog, yo, K1; repeat from *.

ROW 2 AND ALL EVEN-NUMBERED (WRONG-SIDE) ROWS THROUGH 16: Purl.

ROW 3: K1, K1, yo, ssk, K3, K2tog, yo, K2; repeat from *.

ROW 5: K1, *K2, yo, ssk, K1, K2tog, yo, K3; repeat from *.

ROW 7: K1, *K3, yo, (sl2tog, K1, p2sso), yo, K4; repeat from *.

ROW 9: HB, *K2, K2tog, yo, K1, yo, ssk, K2, HB; repeat from *.

ROW 11: K1, *K1, K2tog, yo, K3, yo, ssk, K2; repeat from *.

ROW 13: K1, *K2tog, yo, K5, yo, ssk, K1; repeat from *.

ROW 15: K2tog, *yo, K7, yo, (sl2tog, K1, p2sso); repeat from * to last 9 stitches, yo, K7, yo, ssk.

Repeat Rows 1–16 for pattern.

Knitting the Stole

Note: Begin each row by slipping the first stitch purlwise with yarn in back.

- **SETUP:** Cast on 133 stitches.
- **ROWS 1–12:** Knit.
- **NEXT ROW:** Maintaining a 6-stitch garter stitch border and continuing to slip the first stitch of every row, begin working the Diamond Lace pattern, adding beads as indicated.
- **NEXT ROWS:** Continue until stole measures 78½" (199 cm).
- **NEXT ROW:** Work Row 1 of pattern.
- **NEXT ROWS:** Knit 12 rows.
- Bind off using the tubular bind-off method (see page 153).

●● **ALTERNATE DESIGN IDEA** ●●

A space-dyed yarn lends a more casual feel to the beaded stole. The swatch is knitted in Malabrigo Lace (baby merino), color 135 Emerald, with 8° transparent turquoise hex-cut beads.

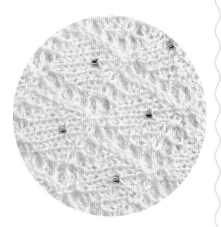

Finishing

- Weave in ends using a tapestry needle.
- Wet stole completely and gently squeeze out excess water.
- Lay the stole on top of towels on a flat surface, shaping and pinning to blocked measurements. Allow to dry completely.

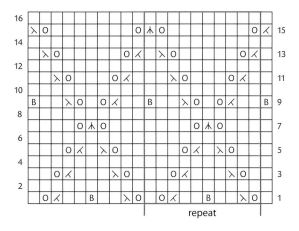

repeat

	Knit on the right side; purl on the wrong side
↘	Slip, slip, knit the 2 slipped stitches together
↗	Knit 2 together
O	Yarn over
B	Hook bead
⋏	Slip 2 together, K1, pass the 2 slipped stitches over

⑦ Putting It All Together

The single project in this last chapter gives you a chance to use all five of the techniques for knitting with beads that are presented in this book. Experiment with different colors and weights of yarn and types and sizes of beads — there's no end to the possibilities here!

Sampler Beaded Bag

This very special small bag is knitted back and forth in one piece and sewn up the sides when completed. The top motif is done with slipstitch bead knitting and the hanging dagger beads are on a carry-along yarn. Then come three rows of bead knitting, followed by a row of cube beads that are hooked, and finally the body of the bag is done with beaded knitting.

Finished Measurements	5" (12.5 cm) at widest × 4" (10 cm) tall
Yarn	Classic Elite Cotton Bam Boo, 52% cotton/48% bamboo, 1.75 oz (50 g)/ 130 yd (119 m) *[Yarn band gauge: 6 stitches = 1" (2.5 cm) on US 5 (3.75 mm) needles]*; Color 3648 Heron Blue, 1 skein
Beads	Size 8° cylinder beads: 808 (25 g) silver-lined crystal; 4mm cube beads: 22 silver-lined crystal; 3.4mm drop beads: 28 silver-lined crystal; 3mm × 11mm dagger beads: 14 clear
Needles	US 5 (3.75 mm) straight and double-pointed needles (two), *or size you need to obtain correct gauge*
Gauge	24 stitches and 40 rows = 4" (10 cm) in stockinette stitch
Other Supplies	Big eye beading needle, 20" (51 cm) cotton/crochet thread for carry-along, tapestry needle, US 8 (1.5 mm) crochet hook
Abbreviations	**HB** hook bead *(see page 126)* **KB** knit with bead *(see page 25)* **PB** purl with bead *(see page 25)* **S1B** slide 1 bead up against needle (S2B=slide 2 beads, etc.) *(see page 50)* **SS1B** slipstitch 1 bead *(see page 76)* **YBB3** bring yarn to back with 1 drop bead, 1 dagger bead, 1 drop bead *(see page 96)* **YFB3** bring yarn to front with 1 drop bead, 1 dagger bead, 1 drop bead *(see page 96)*

Stringing the Beads

- Using a big eye beading needle, string all cylinder beads onto project yarn. Cut cotton/crochet thread in half and string [1 drop bead, 1 dagger bead, 1 drop bead] seven times onto each half.

Knitting the First Slipstitch Motif

- SETUP: With beaded project yarn, use the long-tail method to cast on 25 stitches.
- ROW 1 (RS): Knit.
- ROW 2: Purl.
- ROW 3: Using beads strung on project yarn, K3, *SS1B, K5; repeat from * to last 4 stitches, SS1B, K3.
- ROW 4: P2, *SS1B, P1, SS1B, P3; repeat from * to last 5 stitches, SS1B, P1, SS1B, P2.

- ROW 5: Repeat Row 3.
- ROW 6: Purl.
- ROWS 7 AND 8: Knit.

Knitting the First Carry-Along Motif

- ROW 1 (RS): Knit.
- ROW 2: With project yarn only (do not work beads strung on the project yarn into this section) and 1 piece of beaded cotton crochet thread held together, P1. Holding beaded cotton thread to front (WS), *P2 with project yarn, YBB3 with beaded cotton crochet thread (beads hang on RS), slip next stitch, move beaded cotton crochet thread back to front; repeat from * to last 3 stitches, P2, P1 with yarn and cotton crochet thread held together.
- ROW 3: Knit.
- ROW 4: Purl.
- ROWS 5 AND 6: Knit.

Knitting the First Bead Knitting Motif

- ROW 1 (RS): Using beads strung on project yarn, K1, KB23, K1.
- ROW 2: P1, PB23, P1.
- ROW 3: Repeat Row 1.
- ROW 4: Knit.

Knitting the First Hook Bead Motif

- ROW 1 (RS): Knit.
- ROW 2: Purl.
- ROW 3: Using the cube beads, K2, *HB1, K1; repeat from * to last 3 stitches, HB1, K2.
- ROW 4: Purl.
- ROW 5: Knit, decreasing 1 stitch. *You now have* 24 stitches.

Knitting the Beaded Knitting Motif

- ROW 1 (WS): Using beads strung on project yarn, *K2, S1B; repeat from * to last 2 stitches, K2.
- ROWS 2–6: Repeat Row 1.
- ROW 7 (WS): *K2, S2B; repeat from * to last 2 stitches, K2.
- ROWS 8–29: Repeat Row 7.
- ROWS 30–35: Repeat Row 1.

Knitting the Second Hook Bead Motif

- Repeat Rows 1–4 of Hook Bead Motif, increasing 1 stitch in the first row. *You now have* 25 stitches.

Knitting the Second Bead Knitting Motif

- ROW 1 (RS): Purl.
- ROW 2: P1, PB23, P1.
- ROW 3: K1, KB23, K1.
- ROW 4: Repeat Row 2.
- ROW 5: Purl.

Knitting the Second Carry-Along Motif

- ROW 1 (WS): Purl.
- ROW 2: Knit.
- ROW 3: Purl.
- ROW 4: With project yarn only (do not work beads strung on the yarn into this section) and 1 piece of beaded cotton/crochet thread held together, K1. Holding beaded cotton/crochet thread to back (WS), *K2 with project yarn, YFB3 with beaded cotton/crochet thread (beads hang on RS), slip next stitch, move beaded cotton/crochet thread to back; repeat from * to last 3 stitches, K2, K1 with yarn and cotton/crochet thread held together.
- ROW 5: Purl.

Knitting the Second Slipstitch Motif

- ROW 1 (RS): Purl.
- ROW 2: Purl.
- ROW 3: Knit.
- ROW 4: P3, *SS1B, P5; repeat from * to last 4 stitches, SS1B, P2.
- ROW 5: K2, *SS1B, K1, SS1B, K3; repeat from * to last 5 stitches, SS1B, K1, SS1B, K2.
- ROW 6: Repeat Row 4.
- ROW 7: Knit.

Finishing

- Bind off in knit on wrong side.
- Fold bag in half so that Slipstitch Motifs are at top edges of bag. Sew side seams using a tapestry needle. For handle, pick up 3 stitches at one side seam. Using the two double-pointed needles, *knit all 3 stitches. Without turning work, slide the stitches to the other end of the needle. Pull the working yarn across the back. Repeat from * until handle is 24" (61 cm), or desired length. Bind off. Attach I-cord to bag at opposite side seam. Weave in ends.

ABBREVIATIONS

CA	color A
CB	color B
CC	contrasting color
cm	centimeter(s)
g	gram(s)
K	knit
Kfb	knit in front and back of same stitch
K2tog	knit two stitches together
K3tog	knit three stitches together
m	meter(s)
MC	main color
P	purl
P3tog	purl three stitches together
psso	pass slipped stitch over
RS	right side
ssk	slip one stitch, slip one stitch, knit the two stitches together through their back loops
st(s)	stitch(es)
tbl	through back loop
WS	wrong side
wyib	with yarn in back
wyif	with yarn in front
yo	yarn over

BEAD SIZES

Most beads are measured in millimeters (mm). However, seed beads are measured in *aught* (pronounced like "ought") sizes. The aught symbol we've used in this book looks like the common degree symbol (°), but it can also be written as a numeral with a slash followed by a zero. For example, a size 8 seed bead can be written as 8° or 8/0.

Some sources equate bead sizes with the number of beads that fit side by side per inch. In actuality, seed-bead size is related to the size of the original glass rod that is cut into the bead-size pieces, and there are usually more beads per inch than the size number would indicate. For example, there are usually nine or ten 6° seed beads per inch, not six. (And of course, bead sizes do vary slightly by manufacturer.)

What you can count on, however, is that the smaller (or lower) the bead-size number, the larger the bead: A 6° seed bead is larger than an 8° seed bead, which is larger than an 11° seed bead, and so on.

GLOSSARY

BACKSTITCH

With a threaded tapestry needle, anchor the yarn at the beginning of the seam. *Working from right to left, count over two stitches and pass the needle through both layers from back to front. Then count back one stitch to the right and pass through both layers from front to back. Repeat from * until seam is completed.

BACKWARD LOOP CAST-ON

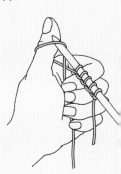

1. Hold the end of the yarn and a needle in your right hand. Hold the working yarn in your left hand.

2. Bring your left thumb over the top, down behind, and up in front of the yarn, creating a loop.

3. Insert needle into loop on thumb as if to knit and slide loop onto needle. You also may use the backward loop cast-on to add stitches to the end of a row of knitting.

CHAIN CROCHET

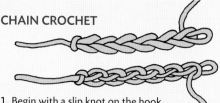

1. Begin with a slip knot on the hook.

2. Wrap yarn over hook and pull a loop through the slip knot.

3. Wrap yarn over hook and pull a loop through the loop on the hook to make a second chain.

4. Repeat for the required number of chain stitches.

KITCHENER STITCH

This grafting technique is used to join two sets of live stitches invisibly. It is most often used for sock toes, but can be used to join shoulder seams or two halves of a scarf.

1. Place the two sets of live stitches to be bound off on separate needles. Hold the needles parallel in your left hand with right sides of the knitted fabric together.

2. Insert the tapestry needle into the first stitch on the front needle as if to knit and slip the stitch off the needle.

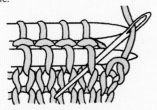

3. Insert the tapestry needle into the next stitch on the front needle as if to purl and leave the stitch on the needle.

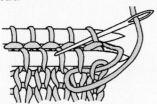

4. Insert the tapestry needle into the first stitch on the back needle as if to purl and slip the stitch off the needle.

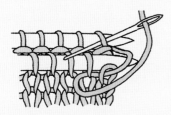

5. Insert the tapestry needle into the next stitch on the back needle as if to knit and leave the stitch on the needle.

6. Repeat steps 2–5 until all stitches have been joined.

KNIT THE KNITS AND PURL THE PURLS

This simply means that you work the stitches as they appear on your needles. For example, if a stitch was knitted on the right-side row, it appears as a purl on the wrong side and should be purled on the wrong-side row.

KNITWISE

When a pattern says "slip the next stitch knitwise" or "slip the next stitch kwise," insert your needle into the next stitch from front to back as if you were going to knit it, then slip it to the right needle without knitting it.

MAKE 1 INCREASE

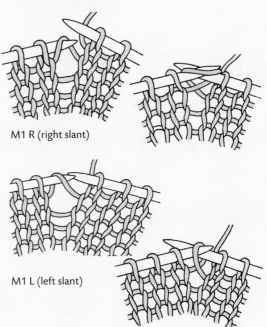

M1 R (right slant)

M1 L (left slant)

This increase is worked into the strand between the current stitch and the next.

1. Work in pattern to where you want to increase.

2. Lift the strand between the two needles and place the lifted strand on the left needle as shown above.

3. Knit or purl the stitch.

MATTRESS STITCH

For a full-stitch seam allowance, work through two horizontal bars on either side of the stitches.

PICK UP AND KNIT

1. With right side facing, insert the needle under both strands of the edge stitch.

2. Wrap the yarn around the needle.

3. Knit the picked-up stitch.

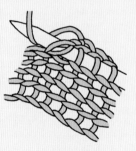

PROVISIONAL CAST-ON

1. Make a slip knot and place it on a crochet hook. Hold your knitting needle on top of a long strand of yarn.

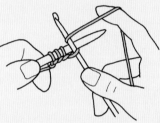

2. Use the crochet hook to draw the yarn over the needle and through the loop on the hook.

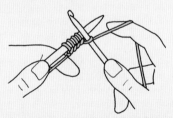

3. Bring yarn behind knitting needle into position as for step 1 and repeat step 2 to cast on another stitch.

Note: If you find it awkward to cast on the first couple of stitches, work a few crochet chain stitches (see page 150) before casting onto the needle so you have something to hold onto.

4. Continue until the last stitch has been cast on, work two or three extra crochet chain stitches without taking the yarn around the knitting needle, and cut the yarn, leaving a 10" (25.5 cm) tail.

5. Draw the tail through the last loop on the hook and pull the tail to close the loop loosely — just enough so the tail can't escape.

6. Remove the scrap yarn when you've finished the knitting by pulling the tail out of the last loop and gently tugging on it to "unzip" the chain. Carefully place the live stitches on a needle, holder, or separate length of scrap yarn as they are released.

PURLWISE

When a pattern says "slip the next stitch purlwise" or "slip the next stitch pwise," insert your needle into the next stitch from back to front as if you were going to purl it, then slip it to the right needle without purling it.

THREE-NEEDLE BIND-OFF

1. Place the two sets of live stitches to be bound off on separate needles. Hold the needles parallel in your left hand with right sides of the knitted fabric together.

2. Insert the tip of a third needle into the first stitch on both needles and knit these two stitches together.

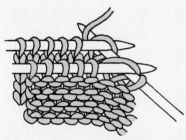

3. Repeat step 2. You now have two stitches on the right needle.

4. Use one of the needles in your left hand to lift the first stitch on the right needle over the second and off the needle as for a regular bind-off. Repeat until all stitches are bound off.

TUBULAR BIND-OFF

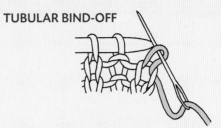

1. Insert threaded tapestry needle knitwise into first stitch and slip it off the needle.

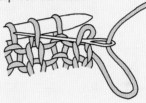

2. Insert tapestry needle purlwise into third stitch and pull yarn through.

3. Insert tapestry needle purlwise into second stitch and slip it off the needle.

4. Insert tapestry needle from back to front between third and fourth stitches, insert it knitwise into fourth stitch, and pull the yarn through.

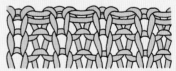

Repeat steps 1–4 until all stitches have been bound off.

BIBLIOGRAPHY

Cooper, Frank. *Oriental Carpets in Miniature: Charted Designs for Needlepoint or What You Will.* Loveland, Colorado: Interweave Press, 1995.

Dubin, Lois Sherr. *The History of Beads: From 30,000 B.C. to the Present.* New York: Harry N. Abrams, Inc., 1987.

Fitzgerald, Diane. *Zulu Inspired Beadwork: Weaving Techniques and Projects.* Loveland, Colorado: Interweave Press, 2007.

Hiatt, June Hemmons. *The Principles of Knitting: Methods and Techniques of Hand Knitting.* New York: Simon and Schuster, 1988.

Kliot, Kaethe. "Knitting and Beads," *Interweave Knits,* Volume II, Number 2 (1997): 44–45.

Poulin-Alfeld, Michelle. "Something Old, Something New," *Interweave Knits,* Volume II, Number 2 (1997): 55.

The Priscilla Bead Work Book. Boston: The Priscilla Publishing Company, 1912.

Rutt, Richard. *A History of Hand Knitting.* London: B.T. Batsford Ltd.; Loveland, Colorado: Interweave Press, 1987.

Thomas, Mary. *Mary Thomas's Knitting Book.* New York: Dover Publications, 1972.

Wolters, Natacha. *Les Perles : Au fil du textile.* Paris: Syros, 1996.

RESOURCES

Beads, Sequins, and Other Supplies

Caravan Beads
www.caravanbeads.com
beads used: Beads for Beads-Go-Sporty Pullover (see page 88), Beady-Eyed Cable Socks (see page 82), Beady Tam (see page 134), Carpet Coasters (see page 32), Colorful Diamonds Gloves (see page 40), Crystal Cardigan (see page 64), Drop-Bead Evening Shell (see page 102), Grape and Berries Pillow (see page 98), Iridescent Beaded Scarf (see page 54), Turquoise Mixed Bag (see page 36), and Zulu Inspired Vest (see page 112) [Beads available wholesale and retail]

Cartwright's Sequins & Vintage Buttons
www.ccartwright.com
paillettes used: Mermaid Shoulder Bag (see page 128)

Ghee's
www.ghees.com
supplies used: Straight hex-open frame for Golden Purse (see page 58)

Toho Shoji
www.tohoshoji-ny.com
beads used: Beads for Golden Purse (see page 58), Magic Mohair Beret (see page 78), and Wedding Stole (see page 138)

The Beadsmith
www.beadsmith.com
[Beads available wholesale to shops]

Yarn

Alpaca with a Twist
www.alpacawithatwist.com
yarns used: Fino for Wedding Stole (see page 138)

Berroco, Inc.
www.berroco.com
yarns used: Lang Yarns Jawoll for Beady-Eyed Cable Socks (see page 82)

Blue Heron Yarns
www.blueheronyarns.com
yarns used: Rayon Metallic for Mermaid Shoulder Bag (see page 128)

Classic Elite Yarns
www.classiceliteyarns.com
yarns used: Cotton Bam Boo for Sampler Beaded Bag (see page 144)

Coats & Clark
www.coatsandclark.com
yarns used: J&P Coats Royale Classic Crochet Thread for Turquoise Mixed Bag (see page 36) and Drop-Bead Evening Shell (see page 102) and J&P Coats Royale Metallic Crochet Thread for Golden Purse (see page 58)

DMC Corporation
www.dmc-usa.com
yarns used: Size 8 perle cotton for Carpet Coasters (see page 32)

Ellie's Reclaimed Cashmere
www.elliesreclaimedcashmere.com
yarns used: Spring Mix for Grape and Berries Pillow (see page 98)

Knit One, Crochet Too, Inc.
www.knitonecrochettoo.com
yarns used: Ambrosia for Iridescent Beaded Scarf (see page 54)

Knitting Fever, Inc.
www.knittingfever.com
yarns used: Debbie Bliss Pure Silk for Crystal Cardigan (see page 64)

Louet Sales
www.louet.com
yarns used: Gems for Beads-Go-Sporty Pullover (see page 88)

Muench Yarns
www.muenchyarns.com
yarns used: GGH Tajmahal for Beady Tam (see page 134)

Peace Fleece
www.peacefleece.com
yarns used: DK for Grape and Berries Pillow (see page 98)

South West Trading Company (SWTC)
www.soysilk.com
yarns used: Bamboo for Drop-Bead Evening Shell (see page 102)

Wagtail Yarns
www.wagtailyarns.com.au
yarns used: 100% Kid Mohair (4 ply) for Magic Mohair Beret (see page 78)

Westminster Fibers, Inc.
www.westminsterfibers.com
yarns used: Rowan 4-Ply Soft for Colorful Diamonds Gloves (see page 40) and Rowan Classic Yarns Silk Wool DK for Zulu Inspired Vest (see page 112)

INDEX

Page numbers in *italics* indicate photographs or illustrations. Page numbers in **bold** indicate charts or tables.

PHOTOGRAPHY AND ILLUSTRATION CREDITS

Front cover photography, main image by © Kate Sears/Sublime Management and small images by © John Polak Photography; back cover photography, all images by © John Polak Photography, except author's image by © Adrien Bisson

Interior photography by © John Polak Photography: 1–9, 11–32, 34–36, 38–40, 42–54, 56, 57 top, 58, 60–64, 66–71, 74–78, 80–82, 84, 85, 88, 90, 94–98, 100, 101 top, 102, 104–108, 112, 114–119, 124–128, 130–134, 136, 138, 140, 141 top, 144, 147; and by © Kate Sears/Sublime Management: 10, 33, 37, 41, 55, 57 bottom, 59, 65, 72, 79, 83, 86, 89, 92, 99, 101 bottom, 103, 109, 113, 123, 129, 135, 139, 141 bottom, 142, 145

Illustrations by Alison Kolesar

Charts by Leslie Anne Charles, LAC Design, with schematics by Ilona Sherratt

ACKNOWLEDGMENTS

It's a pleasure to work with Storey Publishing, and thanks go to editors Gwen Steege and Deborah Balmuth for their encouragement and guidance, and to publisher Pam Art and vice president Dan Reynolds for support of the project.

Thanks to creative director Alethea Morrison and to art director Mary Velgos for making such a lovely book. There is nothing like good editing, and thanks go to Amy Polcyn for her technical eye, to Maria Turner for her copy expertise, and to Kathy Brock for editorial management. Now that the book is made, I'm grateful to Amy Greeman and Jayme Hummer for telling the world about it.

Most especially, thank you, Philippe, for your unending love and support.

ABOUT THE AUTHOR

Judith Durant is the author of *Never Knit Your Man a Sweater** (**unless you've got the ring!*) (Storey Publishing, 2006) and *Ready, Set, Bead!* (Creative Publishing International, 2007); coauthor of *Beadwork Inspired by Art: Impressionism* and *Beadwork Inspired by Art: Art Nouveau* (both with Jean Campbell, Creative Publishing International, 2008) and *The Beader's Companion* (with Jean Campbell, Interweave Press, 1998, revised 2005); and editor of *Luxury Yarn One-Skein Wonders* (Storey Publishing, 2008), *101 Designer One-Skein Wonders* (Storey Publishing, 2007), and *One-Skein Wonders* (Storey Publishing, 2006).

Judith received a BFA in costume design for theater. She worked as a costume artisan for theater and television in New York City before beginning a publishing career with Drama Book Publishers, a publisher of technical theater books. She is a former craft book editor for Interweave Press and a founding editor of *Interweave Knits*. She has contributed designs and articles to *Interweave Knits*, *Beadwork*, and *PieceWork* magazines and had a regular column in *Beadwork* for five years. Her mother taught her to knit when she was eight years old.

Other Storey Titles You Will Enjoy

2-AT-A-TIME SOCKS
by Melissa Morgan-Oakes.
An easy-to-learn new technique to banish
Second Sock Syndrome forever!
144 pages. Hardcover with concealed wire-o.
ISBN 978-1-58017-691-0.

101 DESIGNER ONE-SKEIN WONDERS
edited by Judith Durant.
More patterns for every lonely skein in your stash, from
America's knitwear designers.
256 pages. Paper. ISBN 978-1-58017-688-0.

LUXURY YARN ONE-SKEIN WONDERS
edited by Judith Durant.
The one-skein concept meets luxury fibers, including alpaca,
silk, cashmere, and bamboo — fun, fast, and decadent!
272 pages. Paper. ISBN 978-1-60342-079-2.

NEVER KNIT YOUR MAN A SWEATER*
(*UNLESS YOU'VE GOT THE RING!) *by Judith Durant.*
Smart, good-looking patterns for every stage of your relationship.
184 pages. Paper. ISBN 978-1-5807-646-0.

ONE-SKEIN WONDERS: 101 YARN SHOP FAVORITES
edited by Judith Durant.
One hundred and one projects for all those single skeins
in your stash, collected from yarn shops across America.
240 pages. Paper. ISBN 978-1-58017-645-3.

These and other books from Storey Publishing are available
wherever quality books are sold or by calling 1-800-441-5700.
Visit us at *www.storey.com*.